CULTURES OF THE WORLD

# BELIZE

*Leslie Jermyn*

MARSHALL CAVENDISH
*New York • London • Sydney*

Reference edition reprinted 2001 by
Marshall Cavendish Corporation
99 White Plains Road
Tarrytown
New York 10591

© Times Media Private Limited 2001

Originated and designed by
Times Books International, an imprint of
Times Media Private Limited, a member of the
Times Publishing Group

Printed in Malaysia

*Library of Congress Cataloging-in-Publication Data:*

Jermyn, Leslie.
    Belize / Leslie Jermyn.— Reference ed.
        p. cm. — (Cultures of the world)
    Includes bibliographical references and index.
    ISBN 0-7614-1190-9
    1. Belize—Juvenile literature. [1. Belize.]    I. Title. II.
Series.
F1443.2 .J47 2001
972.82—dc21

                              00-065699
                                CIP
                                 AC

# INTRODUCTION

Belize, or British Honduras as it used to be known, is a fascinating country on the eastern side of the Central American isthmus. It is unique in the region because, unlike its neighbors, it has a British cultural and linguistic tradition instead of a Spanish one. It is a tiny country but does not lack natural and social diversity. Belize is a country of immigrants, past and present. People have come to live here to reap the bounties of nature and sometimes to escape difficult circumstances in their homelands. Belizeans have also become immigrants to other countries, especially the United States. Today, Belize stands as an example of a culturally and ecologically diverse nation adapting to the modern world. In this book, we will explore how Belize became an English-speaking corner of Spanish Central America, learn about the current challenges and problems faced by this tiny country in the global economy, and explore some of its natural and cultural wonders.

# CONTENTS

A Belizean mural.

# CONTENTS

A Garifuna woman.

5

# GEOGRAPHY

BELIZE IS A TINY COUNTRY on the Caribbean side of the Central American isthmus, just south of the Yucatán Peninsula. The country has a coastline of about 174 miles (280 km), and occupies an area of 8,867 square miles (22,965 square km), which is slightly smaller than Massachusetts. Bordered on the north and northwest by Mexico, on the south and west by Guatemala, and on the east by the Caribbean Sea, it is the only Central American country with no access to the Pacific Ocean. The population of Belize is approximately 249,200, and the capital city is Belmopan. Although small, Belize has a diverse landscape and many beautiful geographical features, including the world's second largest barrier reef (180 miles or 290 km long) running parallel to the coast. The country also boasts some rare species of plants and animals.

*Left:* **Boats anchored at San Pedro on Ambergris Cay.**

*Opposite:* **Tourists on an eco-tour along Monkey River.**

*"If the world had any ends, British Honduras (Belize) would certainly be one of them. It is not on the way from anywhere to anywhere else. It has no strategic value. It is all but uninhabited." Aldous Huxley—* Beyond the Mexique Bay.

BELIZE

Feet
16,500
9,900
6,600
3,300
1,650
660
0

Meters
5,000
3,000
2,000
1,000
500
200
0

N

0   10   20   30   40   50 Miles
0      20      40      60      80 Kilometers

MEXICO

Corozal Bay

Cerros

Hondo

New

Ambergris Cay

Cuello

Altun Ha

Cay Caulker

Lamanai

St. George's Cay

Belize

Belize City

Turneffe Islands

Belize   BELMOPAN

Sibun

Caribbean Sea

Half Moon Cay

Xunantunich

Macal River

Range

Stann Creek

Caracol   Doyle's Delight ▲
(3,851 ft / 1,174 m)

Cockscomb Range

Chiquibul
National
Park

Mtn.

Monkey

Maya

Deep

Grande

Gulf of Honduras

Moho

GUATEMALA

Sarstoon

HONDURAS

## PHYSICAL ENVIRONMENT

There are three main physical regions in Belize: the northern lowlands, the southern highlands, and the coastal areas, including offshore islands and atolls. The northern half of the country, where the districts of Corozal, Belize, and Orange Walk are located, is gently undulating, low-lying land. The main rivers here are the Hondo in the far north, and the New, Sibun, and Belize rivers. Most of Belize's agricultural production takes place in this region, and some deciduous forests remain.

The southern half of the mainland of Belize is a highland plateau with the Maya Mountains running up the middle in a north-south direction. The Cockscomb Range is an outcropping of quartz and granite hills in the northeast of this plateau. Belize's highest point used to be Victoria Peak, with a height of 3,681 feet (1,122 m) in the Cockscomb range. However,

Named after the peoples who fled here from the invading Spaniards, the Mayan Mountains are a range of hills which extend about 70 miles (115 km) northeastward from across the Guatemalan border into central Belize.

the most recent survey determines that Doyle's Delight, in the main divide of the Maya Mountains, stands taller by 170 feet at 3,851 feet (1,174 m). Most of the plateau is limestone covered in jungle with many fast-running streams and rivers. The main rivers here are the Monkey, Deep, Grande, Moho, and Sarstoon.

The third region is the most settled and includes the coastal mainland and the small islands and atolls offshore. The longest barrier reef in the Western hemisphere is located 10 to 20 miles (16 to 32 km) offshore, beginning at Ambergris Cay in the north. Islands in Belize are called cays ("KEYS") and make up approximately 212 square miles (549 square km) of the national territory. They run the length of the country, and some lie inside the barrier reef, while others, like the Turneffe Islands, are outside the reef. Given Belize's history as a trading port, most settlement has taken place along the coast and on the cays. Some cays are so small and low-lying that they are nothing more than outcrops of coral, while others, like Cay Caulker and Ambergris, are larger, palm-covered tropical paradises.

## A HOLE IN THE OCEAN FLOOR

About 8 miles (13 km) north of Half Moon Cay in the middle of Lighthouse Reef is a spectacular geological formation called the Blue Hole. This is a limestone sinkhole, a depression created when the top of a cave collapses under the sea. It is more than 300 feet (91 m) across and about 412 feet (126 m) deep and appears as a gorgeous dark blue patch from the surface. The Blue Hole was created about 12,000 years ago, and the stalagmites and stalactites present in the caves leading from the Hole indicate that this part of Belize was dry land during the last Ice Age. Jacques Cousteau made a documentary about it in 1977, and in 1996 the Belizean government made it part of a 1,023-acre (414-hectare) protected natural monument.

## CLIMATE AND SEASONS

Belize is subtropical and enjoys fairly steady temperatures throughout the year. The average temperature is 79°F (26°C) and average humidity about 85%. Generally, the rainy season is June to November, while the dry season is late February to May. Rainfall varies across the country and from year to year. Mean annual rainfall per year in Corozal in the north is 51 inches (1,295 mm), increasing to 74 inches (1,880 mm) for Belize City, and 175 inches (4,445 mm) in the south in Punta Gorda.

Belize is susceptible to storms. Northers are storms that originate in North America and hit Belize with windy, gusty squalls from December to February. Throughout the late summer and fall Belize is also subject to hurricanes. At the opposite extreme, there is the *Mauger* ("MAH-ger") season in August when there is no wind at all. The oppressive heat makes life miserable for Belizeans, who are also at the mercy of insects such as mosquitoes.

*Top:* **A police officer patrols Cay Caulker, which was evacuated after a hurricane.**

*Opposite:* **Lighthouse Reef on Half Moon Cay. Less than 10 feet (3 m) above sea level, Half Moon Cay is teeming with life. Home to colonies of seabirds, numbering in the thousands, this cay's southern beaches are also where the endangered loggerhead and hawksbill turtles lay their eggs.**

Much of the Belizean coast and cays were covered with mangrove trees before people arrived to settle on the land.

## NATURE'S PARADISE

Although tiny, Belize boasts of a large variety of plants and animals (some unclassified) because it is so sparsely settled and cultivated. Some 90% of the land is still covered by some kind of forest: rainforest, pine forest, or mangrove swamp.

In the plant kingdom there are over 4,000 types of flowering plants, including over 250 varieties of orchids, 700 kinds of trees, and hundreds of other types of plants. Some of the more interesting trees include the sapodilla, which produces a gum called chicle, used in chewing gum. The logwood tree was the initial inspiration for permanent settlement of Belize since it produces a purplish-red dye that was extremely important to European textile production from the 16th to the 19th centuries. Belizean lumberjacks have also harvested mahogany trees. These giant trees can grow up to 100 feet (30 m) tall, spreading up to 20 feet (6 m) across the base. A special type of palm called the cohune palm grows in the interior forests. It provides everything from roofing material (from its fronds), to fuel (from the husk of the nut), to buttons and jewelry (from the nut itself). The meat of the nut can also be pounded into flour after the edible oil is extracted. Mangrove trees can be found along the coast and on some cays, where salt water and fresh water intermingle. They can grow to 100 feet (30 m) in height and provide a habitat for many creatures, including crocodiles, crabs, and manatees. Whereas over 90% of the world's mangroves have been cut down, Belize retains over 90% of its original mangrove forests.

Besides an abundance of plant life, Belize is home to some amazing animals. Two kinds of monkeys can be found in mainland forests: the howler monkey and the spider monkey. The howler, called "baboon" by the locals, is a large black monkey with powerful arms and shoulders suited to life in the highest reaches of the forest canopy. Howlers get their name from the sounds they make to mark territory and warn off intruders. Other Belizean mammals include the jaguar, jaguarundi, tapir, and dolphin. Baird's tapir, also known as the "mountain cow," is a large herbivorous animal that lives in the highland forests of southern Belize. The national animal of Belize, it is endangered in most of Central America. These shy, peaceful creatures forage at night and tend to live alone. They can weigh up to 650 pounds (295 kg) but are quite agile in their forest environment. The most famous tapir in Belize is named April, and she lives in the Belize Zoo.

Apart from mammals, Belize is home to hundreds of birds and reptiles. About 540 known species of birds inhabit Belize. The largest flying bird

A black howler monkey. The roars and grunts of the howler monkey are often used on nature soundtracks.

13

in the Western hemisphere is the rare jabiru stork with an average wingspan of 10 feet (3 m). There are only 30 nesting pairs known in Belize. Storks are migratory animals, and the jabiru spends summers in Mexico. Other local birds include colorful toucans, macaws, and parrots. Many reptiles live in the waters and jungles of this small country, including the fer-de-lance snake, known locally as the "yellow-jaw tommygoff." This is a nocturnal pit viper that is equally at home in the cities as in the countryside. This snake can grow up to 8 feet (2 m) in length and is one of the world's deadliest reptiles. Other reptiles include a variety of turtles and the Yucatecan crocodile, known locally as "alligator." These animals live in mangrove forests and can grow to 12 feet (4 m) in length.

**A tourist feeds a tapir in the Belize Zoo. April, the most famous tapir in Belize, is now a mother.**

## ALL MANNER OF TURTLES

Belize has become a refuge for some of the world's most endangered species of turtles. Hunted aggressively by men, the Central American River Turtle, called *hickatee* ("HIK-AH-TEE") locally, is nearly extinct, except in the most remote parts of southern Mexico, northern Guatemala, and Belize. Three other species of sea turtles also use Belizean beaches to lay their eggs: the green, hawksbill, and loggerhead sea turtles.

These turtles have become endangered for a number of reasons. The green turtle has long been hunted to make turtle soup, while the hawksbill's carapace was once used extensively to make tortoiseshell frames for eyeglasses, jewelry, and other decorative items. Trade in tortoiseshell is now outlawed, but the sea turtles are still under threat. Mature females come to shore during the summer to lay their eggs in the sand. By some miracle of nature, these animals find the same beach where they were born some 50 years earlier. However, fences, loud noises, dogs, and people all prevent the females from laying their eggs. Once the eggs are laid, they are then raided by people who eat them as a delicacy. Those that hatch must then make a mad dash for the sea, at the mercy of birds, crabs, and humans. Only about 5% of 100 turtles in a nest make it.

A street scene in Belize City.

## A COUNTRY WITH TWO CAPITAL CITIES

The biggest and busiest of Belize's cities is Belize City. Approximately 54,000 Belizeans live and work there, making it the most populous city in the country. It is located on the coast where the Belize River empties into the Caribbean Sea. Once the capital of British Honduras, it is the oldest urban settlement in the country. Scottish, English, and French pirates and buccaneers built camps here in the 17th century and used the slow-moving Belize River to float logs from the inland forests down to ships waiting at the harbor. These camps formed the basis for the development of Belize Town in the 18th and 19th centuries. At only 18 inches (46 cm) above sea level, the city is highly susceptible to flooding in bad weather and vulnerable to hurricanes off the ocean.

Even before Hurricane Hattie destroyed 75% of Belize City in 1961, there had been talk of moving Belize's capital. Apart from the obvious need to locate government buildings and functions away from the fury of the sea, the people felt that Belize City was becoming squalid and overcrowded. Construction of a new capital began in 1966 at Belmopan, approximately 50 miles (80 km) inland from Belize City. The main government complex was designed to look like a Mayan temple, and the name, Belmopan, combines the "Bel" from Belize and "Mopan" from the name of a group of Mayan Indians. The new capital opened officially in 1970, but the hoped for relocation of people out of Belize City did not take place. Even with the growth of Belmopan as a transportation hub, only two foreign embassies and a few industries have relocated. Today, less than 7,000 people call Belmopan home. It operates as the official capital while most commercial activity remains in Belize City.

A bus station in Belmopan.

# HISTORY

BELIZE IS THE ONLY COUNTRY IN CENTRAL AMERICA with a British colonial heritage rather than a Spanish one. This difference, which resulted from a number of historical quirks, makes it unique in many ways. At the same time, Belize shares its history with its Spanish-speaking neighbors since it was also once governed by the Maya, a sophisticated, indigenous culture that occupied a vast stretch of territory from southern Mexico to Honduras.

## THE MAYAN CIVILIZATION AND BEFORE

The original inhabitants of Belize were hunters and gatherers who had crossed the Bering Strait from Asia around 20,000 B.C. and made their way down from Alaska to populate North, Central, and South America. From

*Left:* **Close-up of ruins at Xunantunich, a prehistoric site in Belize.**

*Opposite:* **The ruins of the ancient Mayan city at Xunantunich.**

about 7,000 B.C. to 2,500 B.C., these nomadic foragers became settled farmers, depending on corn, beans, and squash for their primary subsistence. By 2,500 B.C. the people living in Belize spoke Mayan languages and developed pottery. From then until A.D. 250, the preclassic period, the Maya began to develop social and agricultural practices that provided the foundation for the classic period of Mayan civilization (A.D. 250 to A.D. 900–1000).

During the classic period, Mayan civilization flourished in the Yucatán region of southern Mexico, Guatemala, Belize, and Honduras. Cities were built, some with huge temples and government buildings. Belize boasts the remains of the earliest Mayan settlements and late postclassic ceremonial construction, as well as majestic ruins from the classic period. Cuello, about 3 miles (5 km) west of Orange Walk, is the site of the earliest known Mayan settlement.

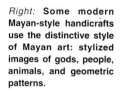

*Right:* **Some modern Mayan-style handicrafts use the distinctive style of Mayan art: stylized images of gods, people, animals, and geometric patterns.**

*Opposite:* **Modern slate carving of the Mayan calendar.**

Mayan leaders were thought to possess both human and godly powers. Mayan society consisted of royalty, merchants, and commoners. The merchants were important since they established a commercial network throughout the Mayan lowlands. Products traded among cities included such luxury goods as obsidian, a volcanic glass used for tools and weapons, jade, animal skins, bird feathers, honey, dried fish, cotton, and cacao.

The Maya were very sophisticated mathematicians and astronomers. Designers of complex systems of agricultural and water management, they also devised a complicated calendar which combined a 365-day solar calendar with a 260-day mystical one. The Mayans calculated the time it takes Venus to go around the sun as 584 days. We now know that it is 583.92 days, so the Mayans were incredibly accurate. They also had a system of hieroglyphic writing with which they recorded their calculations, history, and genealogy.

Near the end of the classic period (A.D. 900), Mayan civilization went into decline. Returning to Guatemala, they established a refuge there and maintained their independence until 1697. Some continued to live in Belize, and sites such as those at Cuello, Cerros, Altun Ha, and Lamanai tell of their enduring presence in the region.

## WHAT HAPPENED TO THE MAYA?

Mayan civilization peaked between A.D. 250 and A.D. 900-1000, when most of the large ceremonial centers, such as Xunantunich, Altun Ha, and Lamanai, flourished. After this time, archaeological evidence shows a dramatic decline in population and the disappearance of Mayan cities throughout the lowlands of Belize, Guatemala, Honduras, and Mexico.

Mayan specialists have pondered the causes for this rather sudden collapse. A number of explanations have been proposed, including climatic changes, hurricanes, earthquakes, and epidemics of disease. Scholars now believe that the Mayan civilization simply grew too rapidly to feed itself. Relying on tropical agriculture limited how much food could be produced and still allow the land to recuperate between plantings. It is suspected that the population grew to a point where there were periodic shortages of food, causing malnutrition and starvation and leaving the elite groups incapable of maintaining control. This eventually led to the dispersion of remaining Mayans away from large urban settlements to smaller isolated villages. Although the collapse of the Mayan civilization may have been a quirk of history, some modern scholars think it has relevance for the modern world. Their argument is that we, too, may be reproducing beyond our ability to feed ourselves. Perhaps we should study the Mayans more closely to learn from their mistakes.

## THE EUROPEANS

The Spanish were the first Europeans to arrive in Belize. In the late 15th century they tried to maintain a monopoly of the Caribbean and Central America, leaving Brazil to the Portuguese. Penetrating Belizean forests to cut logwood (used to make dye), they also tried twice to establish Catholic missions among the Maya in the 17th century but were twice forced to leave the area. Although the Spanish laid claim to Belize, they did not establish an effective government then. Early in the 17th century the Dutch, British, and French arrived on the scene.

British buccaneers established settlements along the coast. There were also British settlements off the coast of Honduras and Nicaragua, but in the 1640s the Spanish expelled the British from these territories. Some of these British adventurers had used the dangerous coastline of Belize to hide their pirate ships from the Spanish, raiding their trading ships from these havens. They moved to the mainland when they were expelled from the Spanish islands. These buccaneers, who had originally stolen logwood from the Spanish ships, started to cut and sell it themselves in the 1650s and 1660s. The demand from the European woolen industry for the dye obtained from logwood kept the British in the Bay of Honduras for at least a century.

Throughout the 18th century, the Spaniards attacked British settlements, forcing them to leave temporarily. However, as the Spanish never settled in Belize, the way remained clear for the British to return to harvest logwood and mahogany from its forests. These settlers became known as

**A hand-colored woodcut of caravels. These were light sailing ships, with three or four masts, much used by the Spanish from the 15th to 17th centuries for long voyages.**

*"White people but look upon it (Belize) as a resting, not an abiding, place, one from which they hope eventually to return enriched to their native soil."* *Archibald Robertson Gibbs*—British Honduras: An Historical and Descriptive Account of the Colony from its Settlement.

the Baymen (referring to the Bay of Honduras). Through a series of treaties between Spain and England, they acquired the right to cut wood as far south as the Sibun River, but Spain retained sovereignty over the area and the British could not farm or govern it. Spain made a final attempt to control the region in 1798 at the Battle of St. George's Cay but were beaten by the Baymen. Belize was proclaimed a colony of British Honduras in 1862 and a crown colony in 1871.

As the British could not control and organize the Maya as a labor force, they imported African slaves in the early 18th century to cut wood and perform domestic chores. Their system of slavery was cruel and oppressive, resulting in four slave revolts and hundreds of runaways to the Yucatán Peninsula, Guatemala, or Honduras. Slavery was abolished throughout the British Caribbean in 1838, but the conditions of inequality continued to affect newly freed African-Belizeans.

Until the middle of the 19th century, white Baymen formed a small elite group who controlled logging, land, and the politics of the settlement of Belize City. These landowners or businessmen were the only ones allowed to attend the Public Meeting when decisions were made, and they could even have the Crown representative sent over from England replaced if they did not agree with his policies. However, by the middle of the century, prices for logwood and mahogany had dropped so far that many of the old Baymen families lost control of their businesses and land. New business interests from England were able to acquire land and establish a new and powerful class in Belize.

At the same time, the Clayton-Bulwer Treaty between Britain and the United States was signed in 1850, stating that Britain would recognize American rights to Central America and withdraw from its colonies there. The Bay Islands of Honduras and the Mosquito Coast in Nicaragua were abandoned by Britain, but due to pressure from London-based businesses, a constitution was created for Belize, then called British Honduras, to make it a formal possession of Britain. The new possession was still not a full colony and had its own Legislative Assembly. It was also responsible for its own budget and military defense. When groups of Maya from Mexico arrived in the north in the 1860s and began to farm near logging lands, the new possession had to fund military expeditions against these usurpers. The Maya were well organized and even managed to take Corozal in 1870. As the colony was still in an economic depression, it could not afford these expenses and thus voted to dissolve the Legislative Assembly, becoming a full Crown Colony of Britain in 1872.

## BUCCANEERS, NOT YOUR AVERAGE PIRATES

We often think of buccaneers as being the same as pirates—maritime thieves of history and legend. However, the term "buccaneer" refers to a special group of people found only in Caribbean history. The word comes from the French words "boucans" and "boucaniers," which refer to open grills used to roast meat and the people who did the roasting, respectively. The boucaniers (or buccaneers as they were called in English), were a group of Europeans (French, English, and Dutch) who made their living hunting wild cattle left behind by the Spanish on the north coast of the island of Hispaniola (modern day Haiti and Dominican Republic). They prepared the meat and then sold it to passing ships in the early 17th century.

Since the buccaneers were hostile to Spain and its colonies, the Spanish sent in soldiers to drive away the cattle that supplied the settlement on Hispaniola in 1640. From that point on, buccaneer settlements sprung up in other parts of the Caribbean, including the Bay Islands of Honduras. English and French governors in the area hired the buccaneers as paid pirates to harass Spanish colonists and ships bound for Europe. One buccaneer, Peter Wallace, was the founder of the first European settlement in Belize. By the end of the 17th century, Spain and England signed a peace treaty, and the buccaneers were no longer given formal support. Many turned to real piracy or found other means of livelihood, such as logging.

George Price's campaign headquarters in Belize City.

## INDEPENDENCE AT LAST

At the end of the 19th century, Belize was still largely dependent on forestry. Experiments with other cash crops such as coffee, sugar, and bananas had failed. Belizean-born businessmen and women were forming important ties with American companies and becoming more influential than the British-born businessmen. For example, in the early 20th century Belize began harvesting chicle for sale to Wrigley's in the United States. Belize's economy became increasingly dependent on the United States rather than on Britain. The Great Depression of the 1930s marked the beginning of the end of British dominance over Belize. During the Depression, prices fell for Belize's main exports, mahogany and chicle, creating unemployment and poverty. This was aggravated by a hurricane in 1931 that destroyed Belize City and left most people homeless. The British government's response to the economic and natural disasters was slow and inadequate. Belizean workers and the poor organized themselves politically and formed groups such as the Laborers and Unemployed Association, pushing for reforms in labor law and an awakened political consciousness among Belize's working majority. The People's United Party (PUP) was formed in 1950 under the leadership of George Price. The PUP was anti-British and demanded independence. In 1964 British Honduras was granted self-government and a new constitution. When the PUP won the 1965 elections, Price was elected Premier. British Honduras was renamed Belize in 1973 and, on September 21, 1981 Belize became a fully independent member of the British Commonwealth of Nations.

## CONFLICT WITH GUATEMALA

No history of Belize is complete without a review of the long dispute with Guatemala over the sovereignty of Belizean territory. When the Spanish empire disintegrated in the 1820s, its independent republics claimed sovereign rights over Spain's relinquished territories. Both Mexico and Guatemala made claims on Belize. Mexico dropped its claims in 1893, but Guatemala has persisted with its claims.

**A British army soldier talking to Belizean children.**

The dispute was aggravated by a treaty signed in 1859 between Britain and Guatemala. To the British, this treaty merely settled the boundaries of Belize as an area under British dominion; but the Guatemalans would accept British sovereignty only under certain conditions, the main one being British aid to build a road from Guatemala City to the Caribbean coast. However, this road was never built, and in 1945 Guatemala adopted a constitution stating that Belize was the twenty-third department of Guatemala. Britain, Guatemala, and Belize have been negotiating this issue ever since, with talks occasionally degenerating into threats of military aggression.

A major turning point came when Belize obtained international support from the United Nations, which paved the way for Belize's independence on September 21, 1981. However, Guatemala is not reconciled to this, and a British garrison remains in Belize to strengthen the tiny Belize Defense Force. In 1982 the United States also agreed to station troops in Belize if the British withdrew. Although there is probably little real threat of a Guatemalan invasion, this dispute leaves Belize vulnerable along its longest border.

# GOVERNMENT

BELIZE'S HISTORY AS AN INDEPENDENT country is short, dating back only to 1981. Its structure of government is based on the British parliamentary system, and its legal system is based on the common law system in England. The Queen of England is the head of state, and Belize continues to be dependent on the British for its defense against Guatemala.

## STRUCTURES OF GOVERNMENT

The first constitution of 1981 established Belize as a constitutional monarchy. That means that the Queen of England, currently Elizabeth II, is recognized as the nominal head of state. Her representative in Belize is the governor-general, a Belizean national whose functions are mainly ceremonial. The current governor-general is Sir Colville N. Young.

*Left:* **A political placard speaks against Guatemalan claims on Belizean land.**

*Opposite:* **The courthouse in Belize City.**

The effective leader of Belize is the prime minister, who is the leader of the party that wins a majority in the House of Representatives. The governor-general appoints the prime minister, based on the outcome of elections. The prime minister then appoints the cabinet. There are 28 seats in the House, and these are divided into constituencies based on population and divided among Belize's six districts. In addition to the House of Representatives, there is an eight-member senate. Of these eight senators, five are appointed by the prime minister, two by the leader of the opposition party, and one by the Belize Advisory Council (a body of at least six members appointed by the governor-general).

Bills are proposed by the prime minister and his or her cabinet. Cabinet members act as ministers and can be drawn from either the House or the senate. There are 16 ministries in Belize today: Agriculture; Attorney General's Office; Economic Development; Education and Public Service;

**The former Government House in Belize City.**

Finance; Foreign Affairs; Health and Sports; Home Affairs and Labor; Housing, Urban Development and Cooperatives; National Security; Natural Resources; Public Works; Public Utilities, Transport, and Communications; Tourism; Trade and Industry; and Youth Development, Human Resources, and Women's Affairs. When the cabinet passes a bill with a majority, it is sent to the senate to be ratified in another vote. The last step is for the governor-general to sign the bill into law. The government is formed for a maximum of five years, and the same prime minister can be elected for more than one term.

There are Summary Jurisdiction Courts for criminal cases and District Courts for civil cases in each of Belize's districts. Appeals can be taken to the Supreme Court, which is independent of the national government. After a Supreme Court decision, there is a possibility for appeal in the Court of Appeal. Absolute authority rests with the Privy Council in England. The governor-general, in consultation with the prime minister, appoints justices to the Supreme Court, but they are expected to remain neutral and avoid party politics.

In addition to the national government, there are also elected town boards with seven members for each district. Belize City has a nine-member City Council, and the towns of San Pedro and Benque Viejo del Carmen also have their own boards. Local elections are held every three years. These municipal governments work with village councils and rely on income from property taxes, trade licenses, and national government handouts. Some Mayan villages also have a mayor with limited powers.

Mayors of Cayo district.

## *MILITARY AND POLICE*

The Belizean Defense Force (BDF), formed in 1978, consists of about 1,000 soldiers, 50 marines, and a 15-member air wing. Until 1989 the BDF was under the command of a British officer. In 1989 a Belizean officer was appointed to head the BDF for the first time in Belize's short history as an independent country. In 1995 the Ministry of National Security was created to advise the government on national security matters. There are no longer British officers serving in the BDF, although Belize still relies on training facilities in the United States, Canada, and Britain. Local policing is done by the Belize Police Force (BPF). This force is not well organized, and there is some dissatisfaction with the way they control crime. Recently, the BDF and BPF have been cooperating to fight urban crime and drug smuggling, two of the most serious internal defense problems.

**Policemen in Belize City.**

## POLITICAL PARTIES

There are two main political parties in Belize, the People's United Party (PUP) and the United Democratic Party (UDP). Between them, they have controlled the government since self-government and the formation of the Legislative Assembly in 1964. The PUP was the first political party in Belize and was formed in 1950 to represent those who wanted independence from Britain. It originally relied on the support of labor, but since 1964 it has broadened its base to include Belizeans of all classes. The PUP has been, until recently, the personal forum for George Price, one of Belize's most prominent and influential politicians. Generally speaking the PUP is thought to be the more center-left of the two main parties and has won every election since independence in 1981 except two (1984, 1993), including the most recent in 1998 under the leadership of Said Musa.

People's United Party (PUP) election board in San Pedro on Ambergris Cay.

The newspaper, the *Belize Billboard*, is the official voice of the PUP.

The UDP was formed in 1973 as a combination of three other political parties: National Independence Party, People's Development Movement, and the Liberal Party. Originally, the main platform of the UDP was to oppose independence and the way the PUP was handling the dispute with Guatemala. By the time the UDP won their first election in 1984, under the leadership of Manuel Esquivel, their platform had become more comprehensive, including support for foreign investment and private sector solutions to economic problems. This was a significant election as Price was replaced by Esquivel as Belize's second prime minister. The UDP is considered to be more conservative than the PUP and has close ties with the United States. The UDP's official newspaper is the *People's Pulse*.

The PUP and UDP, both committed to capitalist development, are not clearly divided on policies or support. All classes of people and regions of the country support both parties. Belizeans may choose which party to vote for based on the traditions in their family or on locally important current issues, but they do not choose between radically different political platforms.

# GEORGE PRICE, FATHER OF THE NATION

George Cadle Price (photo below right) is Belize's George Washington. From a middle-class background, he was educated at Belize's elite secondary school, St. John's College. His first choice of career was the Catholic Church, and he studied with the Jesuits in the United States in the 1930s. When he returned to Belize in 1942, he worked closely with Robert Turton, the Creole chicle millionaire, who was an elected member of the Legislative Council at that time. Price was inspired to enter politics and won a seat on the Belize City Council in 1947. A central figure in national politics ever since, he formed the People's United Party (PUP) in 1950 and led Belize's independence movement. He was often criticized for maintaining total control of the PUP but is also highly regarded for his honesty, integrity, and incorruptibility. The man in power when Belize gained internal control of the government in 1964 and total independence in 1981, he is thought of as the Father of the Nation.

Price is an eclectic and pragmatic politician, maintaining his preeminent position for longer than any other national leader in the region.

**Prime Minister Musa officiating Cashew Festival celebrations.**

## *CURRENT POLITICS AND NEW LEADERS*

For the first time since its creation, the PUP is led by someone other than George Price. Said Musa became the new prime minister when the PUP won the government back from the UDP during the election in 1998. Musa is an experienced politician. His campaign agenda in the last election has improved the economy and reduced the burden on Belize's poor and unemployed. Musa reduced a 15% value-added tax that his predecessor, Manuel Esquivel, had imposed, replacing it with lower income, sales, and property taxes. To reduce government spending, Radio Belize was closed, and other government sectors may be sold to private companies. Apart from ongoing economic problems, the main issue that Musa has to deal with is violent crime, which is on the increase in cities, and which is related, at least in part, to drug trafficking.

## OLD SYMBOLS FOR A NEW NATION

The flag of Belize celebrates its history as an English protectorate and as a wood-producing country. The center of this dark blue flag portrays the coat of arms of British Honduras, granted by royal warrant in 1907. The shield of the coat of arms is divided into three parts: the left-hand side contains a squaring ax and paddle crossed; the right-hand side contains a beating ax and saw crossed; and the bottom shows a ship in full sail. The axes and saw stand for the tools used to fell trees, and the paddle and ship indicate the way logs were brought from the interior to the coast down the rivers and then transported across the Atlantic Ocean to England. On either side of the shield stand two workers, one holding an ax and one holding a paddle. Behind the shield is the crest, a mahogany tree, and below it is the motto in Latin: *Sub Umbra Floreo* ("Under the Shade I Flourish"). An olive wreath, a traditional symbol of peace, surrounds the coat of arms.

*Being small, Belize's diplomatic affairs are still mainly handled by British embassies and consulates. Belize has diplomatic posts in the following countries: Canada, Germany, Guatemala, Mexico, United States, and United Kingdom.*

# ECONOMY

BELIZE'S ECONOMY KEEPS evolving as it tries to find its niche in the global market. Being so small, it remains dependent on other countries to invest and develop the economy, as well as to buy Belizean goods. Belize used to depend almost entirely on the export of timber. However, agriculture and fishing have become more important since the 1960s. Belize has also become a service economy with about 65% of its gross domestic product and over 50% of workers employed in tourism, construction, banking, communications, transportation, and community services. Drugs, such as marijuana, are also illegally grown in Belize for export to the United States. Most industry is based on agriculture, such as flour milling, and the production of citrus concentrate and animal feed. A small industrial sector produces goods for local consumption, such as beer, cigarettes, soft drinks, furniture, and construction materials.

*Left:* **A Mennonite furniture shop owner.**

*Opposite:* **A corner grocer shop in Stann Creek. Shops in Belize are usually stocked with both local and imported food.**

Transporting sugarcane in Belize City.

## *FORESTRY AND AGRICULTURE*

The export of timber has been the basis of the Belizean economy for many years, but today forest products are more in demand. Forest products such as furniture, chewing gum, and power and telephone poles are made from mahogany logs, chicle, and pine lumber.

Since the 1970s, agricultural products, particularly sugar, have been the leading exports and earners of foreign currency for Belize. More than one-fourth of the population is engaged in agriculture. Sugarcane is grown in the districts of Corozal and Orange Walk, and Belize exports sugar to the United States and the European Community. Other exports include bananas, citrus fruits (oranges, pomelos, and grapefruit), cacao, and seafood products. Citrus fruits and bananas are grown mainly in the Stann Creek and Cayo areas, south and west of Belize City. Bananas are grown in the southern regions of Stann Creek and Toledo, following a government initiative in the early 1970s to improve export earnings and relieve poverty in this region.

Large companies who employ thousands of Belizeans, as permanent, temporary, or seasonal workers own most of the farms growing products for export. There are 59,000 acres (23,777 hectares) of land planted in sugarcane in northern Belize (Corozal and Orange Walk) owned by 5,000 farmers. Another 40,000 acres (16,120 hectares) of land is under citrus cultivation. Hummingbird Hershey Company, part of Hershey Foods Corporation, started a small cacao plantation in 1977 and also buys a percentage of its cacao from local, small-scale farmers. Currently, other products, such as peanuts, mangoes, and pawpaws, are being tried.

Laborers at work near the Southern Highway.

Belizeans also produce food for their own consumption. The two main crops are rice and kidney beans. Belize exports beans but has to import rice. Other locally produced and consumed products include beef, pork, chicken, milk, eggs, and corn. Belize is self-sufficient in milk and chicken, largely due to the efforts of the Mennonite communities, which have improved local agricultural practices.

About 30% of adult Belizeans work in agriculture either as farm laborers or small, independent farmers. Most of the high-income earning products like sugar, citrus, and bananas are grown by large companies. Cutting sugarcane is one of the worst jobs in the world, since the cane fields are full of snakes and rats, and the leaves on the cane are razor sharp. Citrus pickers are generally underpaid and abused by employers. Nevertheless, many laborers come from nearby Spanish-speaking countries just for the picking season from October to March.

## FROM CITRUS PLANTATION TO ENVIRONMENTAL RESERVE

The Rio Bravo Conservation Area in northwest Belize could have been one large citrus fruit plantation were it not for the efforts of people in the United States and Europe. Five hundred thousand acres (201,500 hectares) of land was sold to Coca-Cola in 1983 by the Belizean owner of Belize Estate and Produce Company, Barry Bowen. Coca-Cola had plans to turn this large expanse of jungle into a fruit plantation. The Massachusetts Audobon Society and the International Friends of the Earth opposed this plan and organized a boycott of Coca-Cola products in Europe. The campaign was so effective that Coca-Cola decided not to develop the area and instead has committed 250,000 acres (100,750 hectares) to the Rio Bravo reserve. Since then, the reserve has continued to operate using private contributions, many of which are organized through the Massachusetts Audobon Society. The reserve is managed by a nonprofit Belizean organization called Program for Belize and is one of the many tourist sites around the country. This is one example of how Belizeans and non-Belizeans are working to preserve the natural environment in Belize.

# FISHING

Belize's main marine exports are shrimp, lobster tails, and conch. Fishermen are organized into cooperatives in Belize, which means they get more of the profits than if they were employed by a big company. The cooperatives are given exclusive rights to harvest the sea, and because every fisherman is also an owner of the cooperative, he earns a higher price for his catch. Unfortunately, there has been a decline in the number of exportable fish due to overfishing in the last 20 years. In the early 1990s Belize began to farm shrimp rather than rely on trawling in the sea. Farmed shrimp has become an important income-earner, although it has a negative environmental impact, as the farms are built in destroyed mangrove forest areas. Hopefully, the fishing cooperatives will find a way to diversify or to allow the lobster and conch to replenish their numbers.

Garifuna fishermen at work.

## A SERVICE ECONOMY

Belize's biggest tourist attractions are its forests and jungles, the barrier reef and cays, and Mayan ruins such as Caracol, Xunantunich, and Lamanai. However, the biggest hotels and tour operators are not Belizean-owned, and locals are employed mainly for unskilled work like cleaning rooms. As tourists become more aware of the importance of supporting local enterprises, this may change. The Belizean government has promoted tourism over the last 30 years and has become more willing to set aside land for nature parks and reserves. Although this occasionally leads to conflicts with local farmers, given the importance of tourism to the economy, this practice will probably continue.

**Tourists on a river ride through the mangroves.**

## ECO-TOURS AND ECO-EXPORTS

One of Belize's largest income-earners is tourism. If Belize's beautiful forests, the main draw for tourists and the habitat for an unrivalled variety of wildlife, are destroyed, one of the country's most important industries will disappear.

One solution for this is eco-tourism, which emphasizes the protection of natural environments and preservation of local cultures. Another solution is the harvesting of natural products without the felling of trees. Both Belizean and foreign-owned companies have started this practice and export ecologically and environmentally friendly products from the rainforest, such as natural chewing gum from chicle, cashew candy, dried jungle fruits, coconut soap, and cohune-nut jewelry and buttons. A side benefit of this new practice is that local residents are usually employed to do the harvesting.

An antidrug billboard at the Belize Industrial Park.

## INFORMAL AND ILLEGAL ECONOMIES

Belize has a flourishing black market. This includes consumer items imported from Mexico and the United States, such as soft drinks, cars, and rum, as well as foreign currency. Black market activities are harmful to the government but give unemployed and poorly paid Belizeans a chance to make enough money to survive. More harmful to Belizeans is the illegal trade in drugs. In the 1980s Belize became a producer and exporter of marijuana. The United States Drug Enforcement Agency (DEA) sponsored programs to spray marijuana fields with pesticides, and by the end of the 1980s much less marijuana was being produced. The new problem in the 1990s was cocaine, and its by-product, crack. The DEA has been pressuring the Belizean government to increase drug enforcement activities, but due to widespread corruption among police and government officials, there has never been a successful conviction against a major Belizean trafficker. Both the American and British governments have offered assistance in the form of training and equipment.

## TRADE

Belize's main trading partners are the United States, United Kingdom, European Union, Canada, and Mexico. Its main exports are agricultural products such as sugar, citrus fruit concentrate, bananas, and seafood. Being a small country means that Belize must rely on preferential trade agreements in order to compete with larger producers in regional markets. For example, the United States buys a percentage of Belizean sugar at a price much higher than that on the open market. Certain Belizean exports, such as clothing, are produced in special export processing zones, where foreign companies can set up small factories without paying taxes on their earnings. This keeps the cost of the product low for the consumer.

With a small manufacturing base, Belize must import much of its clothing and appliances, as well as transportation and other equipment. Belize also imports food, industrial chemicals, petroleum, and beverages. Hence, the cost of living is higher in Belize than in neighboring countries.

Timber being loaded for export at an industrial port in Belize City.

Belizeans boarding a bus to Benque Viejo del Carmen.

## *TRANSPORTATION AND ENERGY*

Since the decline of forestry in the 1950s, roads have become more important. Whereas loggers could use rivers to float their products to the ports, sugar and citrus growers need roads to truck their goods to markets and ports. The first paved road connected Belize City with the Mexican border in the north and is called, appropriately, the Northern Highway. Next to be built was the Western Highway that connects Belize City and Belmopan with Benque Viejo del Carmen on the Guatemalan border. More recently, the Hummingbird Highway from Belmopan to Dangriga was constructed, followed by a new Southern Highway from Dangriga to Punta Gorda. As of 1998, there was a total of 1,784 miles (2,872 km) of highway in Belize, of which only 265 miles (427 km) were paved. With the help of foreign aid, the main airport, the Philip Goldson International Airport, was expanded and renovated in 1990, and a new port built at Big Creek to handle banana and citrus exports. Other ports are Belize City, Punta Gorda, and Corozal. There has also been dramatic improvement in

## Transportation and Energy

Belize's telecommunications, due in part to the government selling this off to the private sector. As a result, Belize has the best telecommunications infrastructure in Central America. It is hoped that these advancements will contribute to economic expansion in the future and improve career prospects for Belizeans.

Belize relies on imported petroleum to fuel its transportation systems both on land and at sea, and on other forms of power for electricity. In 1991 all taxes on imported solar and wind energy devices were dropped to encourage people to use alternative sources of energy. In 1993 construction of a hydroelectric project on the Macal River in Cayo district was started; this project was completed in 1995. Prospecting for petroleum off the coast of Belize has not located any major reserves. However, there are plans to buy electricity from Mexico to supplement local production.

A shipyard in Belize City.

# BELIZEANS

BELIZE HAS A VARIETY OF cultural and linguistic traditions that came from migrant cultures. Through the years, these different cultures have been modified and localized by the immigrants or their descendents. Many Belizeans are of mixed racial ancestry.

## CREOLES

Creolization in Belize is a complex synthesis of African and British traditions. The Creoles are descendents of African slaves brought to the Caribbean during the 18th and early 19th centuries and British settlers, as well as subsequent African immigrants. The Creoles in Belize have modeled their culture on the British. Most speak formal English but use a Belizean creole English at home and in informal situations.

*Above:* **A Creole fisherman cleaning a conch.**

*Opposite:* **Young girls in the district of Cayo.**

The African slaves in Belize were used mainly in logging, unlike those in other parts of the Carribean who worked on plantations. Some slaves did domestic work, while others farmed. Although the African slaves came from many different African peoples, most of their cultures emphasized the importance of religion, and their religious leaders were influential people. The religious leaders were also healers, judges, and teachers. Creoles now occupy a disproportionate number of government and police jobs. They also work in urban occupations on the waterfront, in service industries, and have established small farms and villages. They are largely concentrated in the coastal Belize District, in particular Belize City, which has about half of Belize's Creole community. Since independence, the Creoles have been the dominant culture in Belize, and tensions have arisen between them and the mestizos who speak Spanish.

A mestizo child in a dory.

## MESTIZOS

The term "mestizo" refers generally to any person of mixed blood. In Central and South America it refers more specifically to someone of combined Indian and European heritage. The Spanish-speaking mestizos first arrived in Belize in the thousands in the mid-19th century, following the outbreak of the Caste War in Yucatán between 1847 and 1853. Their numbers almost tripled the tiny population of Belize, which soared from 9,809 in 1845 to 25,635 in 1861.

These early mestizo immigrants tended to stay in rural areas, particularly in northern and western Belize and on cays such as Ambergris and Cay Caulker. They are the backbone of agricultural production. Their numbers have grown tremendously in the last 20 years, from the influx of refugees from war-torn countries such as El Salvador, Nicaragua, and Guatemala. There are now tensions between the mestizos and the English-speaking Creoles over the identity of Belize—is it an English-speaking Caribbean country or a Spanish-speaking Central American nation?

## MAYAN INDIANS

Mayans first came to Belize in A.D. 100, probably from the highlands of Guatemala and El Salvador. They consistently resisted British rule, and their numbers gradually dwindled; they were either chased out or were killed by European diseases or by the British. Modern Mayans are mainly immigrants from Guatemala and Mexico who fled their homes for a variety of reasons. There are three different groups of Maya represented in modern Belize, each with their own language and cultural traditions.

A Mayan Indian boy.

The first group to arrive in Belize were the Yucatec Maya who fled the Caste Wars in southern Mexico in the middle of the 19th century. They settled in northern Belize in the districts of Corozal and Orange Walk. The Mopan Maya live in the Cayo and Toledo districts. They arrived from Guatemala in 1886, fleeing forced labor and taxation by Guatemalan authorities. The biggest Mopan settlement is San Antonio in Toledo. Mopan continue to practice subsistence agriculture growing beans, corn, and roots but are now also producing honey, cacao, and rice for the cash economy. The third group are the Kekchí Maya who migrated to Belize from the Verapaz region of Guatemala to escape slavery at the hands of German coffee growers. They live in about 30 small communities in the Toledo district and are the poorest ethnic group in Belize. They still practice a subsistence agriculture known as slash and burn or *milpa* ("MEEL-pah"). Like the Mopan, the Kekchí produce crops like rice, citrus fruits, and cacao for sale.

The total number of Belizean Maya has increased in the 20th century as a result of further emigration from Guatemala. Today, some Mayan

**A Mopan Mayan girl and her brother.**

groups, particularly those in the more remote southern regions, are organizing themselves to protect their culture and way of life. Considered inferior by the mestizos and Creoles, Mayans are counteracting this by pressurizing the government to establish a Maya Institute and a Maya Land Trust: an area of 500,000 acres (201,500 hectares) dedicated to the Mayan people.

## GARIFUNA

The Garifuna, formerly called Black Caribs, are a unique culture descended from the Carib Indians and Africans in the eastern Caribbean in the 18th century. Their language is based on Carib, but most can speak either standard English or Spanish in addition to their native tongue. Their music and dance, on the other hand, are chiefly African in origin. Traditionally fishermen, the Garifuna are settled mainly along the southern coast, at places such as Dangriga, Punta Gorda, and Barranco. Garifuna have also worked as farmers and laborers. They are famous for their linguistic abilities and are now employed in teaching and government jobs. Under the British, the Garifuna were treated as illegal squatters and prohibited from owning land. They were thought to be inferior and primitive, much like the Mayans. In the last 20 years the Garifuna have been making efforts to celebrate and preserve their distinct culture and are hoping to introduce the Garifuna language to the national school system. They call themselves Garinagu rather than Garifuna, but this name has not yet been adopted by people outside Belize.

## GARIFUNA ORIGINS

The origin of the Garifuna, formerly known as Black Caribs, is fascinating. The Carib peoples were the indigenous groups that lived in the Caribbean and along the northern coast of the South American mainland. Farmers, hunters, and fishermen, they migrated to the Caribbean islands where they traded with the Arawaks, sometimes raiding their settlements and taking their women as wives. The resulting mixture of Carib and Arawak formed the Island Caribs. The Island Carib population was depleted by hostile attacks from Europeans and disease by the 16th century. However, a large group of Caribs survived this genocide and continued to live on the island of St. Vincent. In 1635 two Spanish ships carrying African slaves shipwrecked near St. Vincent. The Island Caribs sheltered the African survivors who intermarried with the Caribs, producing the Black Caribs. Throughout the 18th century, escaped slaves from all over the Caribbean added to their numbers, staunchly resisting European efforts to control and enslave them. Finally, in 1797 the British rounded up the Black Caribs and shipped them to Roatán, one of the islands off the coast of Honduras. From there, Black Caribs began to settle along the coast of Central America from modern day Bluefields in Nicaragua to Dangriga in Belize. On November 19, 1823 a large group of Black Caribs escaping the civil war in Honduras joined a small settlement at present-day Dangriga. This day is celebrated by Belizean Garifuna as Settlement Day.

**An East Indian shop-keeper.**

## EAST INDIANS

East Indians have a long history in Belize, starting from the 1840s when tens of thousands of East Indians were contracted to work in the Caribbean British colonies. Many sugar plantations needed laborers at that time, so a system of indentured labor was introduced. Under this system, laborers were encouraged to come to the Caribbean to work for a "master" for a certain number of years, after which they were free to work as they pleased. However, circumstances often forced these laborers to become "re-indentured." Thousands of Indians agreed to come over to the Caribbean, as they were unemployed and often starving due to droughts at home. When their labor contracts were up, many stayed. Some went to the short-lived American settlement at Punta Gorda to work on the rice and sugar plantations, while others were contracted as sugar workers around Orange Walk, Corozal, and Toledo. East Indians have largely mixed with the Creoles, but their descendents can still be found at Calcutta in the Corozal District and Forest Home in the Toledo District.

## MENNONITES

Mennonites started arriving in Belize after 1958 when they were granted exemption from military service and any compulsory insurance or welfare schemes. Arriving from Mexico and Canada, they were granted permission by the government to establish three colonies at Blue Creek, Shipyard, and Spanish Lookout.

Mennonites are Protestant Christians and related to the Anabaptists. Mennonites are named after Menno Simons, a Dutch priest who consolidated and institutionalized the work initiated by moderate Anabaptist leaders. They do not pay taxes, join armies, or send their children to state schools. Refraining from voting in national affairs, they also do not accept public office. In economic affairs, however, they are active and successful, mostly in the production and sale of poultry and dairy products, honey, and handmade furniture. Their communities live on a collective form of agriculture, speak German, and remain culturally distinct from the rest of Belizean society.

## *"ANYTHING GOES"*

Over the course of its history, Belize has become home to a wide range of peoples with distinct cultures and languages. Although there are tensions and differences, the general attitude has been "anything goes," and there has been little direct racial or ethnic violence. At present, no one group is in complete control of the future of the country, and one of Belize's biggest challenges is to forge a national identity out of the many strands that make up the Belizean tapestry.

To add to the cultural and linguistic potpourri of Belize, there are still white Creoles (descended from British settlers) and new white American

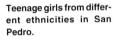

**Teenage girls from different ethnicities in San Pedro.**

immigrants living in Belize. Recent American immigrants have specialized in developing tourism, particularly in the cays, and are largely responsible for putting Belize on the travel map. In the late 1980s and 1990s the government also promoted immigration from Chinese countries such as Hong Kong and Taiwan. Although there has been much criticism of this practice, visas to live and work in Belize, and even passports, have been for sale for US$25–35,000 per person. These Asian migrants invest in Belize in order to gain citizenship and be closer to the United States—the ultimate destination for many. Some, however, wish to make Belize their home and have built communities and schools in the Belize River Valley while maintaining their native languages.

## FAMOUS BELIZEANS

**"Lady Smuggler"** Although her real identity is unknown, this woman worked as a smuggler during the years of Prohibition in the United States. She was the captain of her own ship and made regular trips from Belize to Mexico with rum for shipment into the United States. Her crew respected and obeyed her and even Mexican officials feared her. She was one of the many powerful Belizean women who played a part in Belize's long and colorful history.

**Peter Wallace** was a Scottish sea captain. He was thought to be the first European to anchor his ships inside the barrier reef that runs along Belize's coast. He landed near the mouth of the Belize River and founded a base camp in 1638, which later became Belize City.

**Marcos Canul** and other Maya fled the civil war in Mexico in the 1850s to settle in northern Belize. They chose land beyond the control of the logging companies and began to farm as they had done in Mexico. When the British tried to oust them, Canul led attacks on mahogany camps and

*"The culture of British Honduras developed around groups that had fled persecution elsewhere—slaves, Mennonites, victims of the Caste Wars of Yucatán, and indigenous groups such as the Caribs and Maya."* Anne Sutherland—The Making of Belize: Globalization on the Margins.

settlements in the area. He was finally killed in the Mayan attack at Orange Walk in 1872. Without his brilliant leadership, the Maya people would have been forced to give up their independence and live on reservations. **Sharon Matola** is well-known for her work in starting and maintaining the Belize Zoo, west of Belize City. A former trainer of circus lions, she was also an assistant to a nature filmmaker. When he no longer needed his animal "stars," he told Matola to abandon the jaguars, peccaries, and other animals. Instead, Matola started an informal zoo and spent thousands of hours trying to raise money to feed and house the animals. More than just a collection of cages, her zoo is educational and, together with her children's books about nature, has changed the attitude of Belizean children toward their environment. Matola is also an active campaigner for the rights and protection of native Belizean animals and their natural habitat from the disruptive influences of land redevelopment and urbanization. She received a Whitley Award in 1998 for her work in protecting the scarlet macaw of Belize. Matola spearheaded a field research program and a complementary education program to save this bird, one of the prime victims of the illegal pet trade.

## ETHNIC GROUPS IN BELIZE

A government census taken in 1991 found the following breakdown by ethnic group:

| | |
|---|---|
| Mestizo | 44% |
| Creole | 30% |
| Maya (Amerindian) | 11% |
| Garifuna | 7% |
| Others | 8% |

(includes Asians, German Mennonites, and others of European descent.)

## THE BELIZE ZOO

Started in 1983 by Sharon Matola (photo above), the Belize Zoo and Tropical Education Center was set up to provide a home for wild animals that had been used in the making of documentary films. Soon after the "backyard" zoo opened, it became evident that Belizean visitors were unfamiliar with the different species of wildlife that shared their country. This led to the formation of the Tropical Education Center.

Today, the zoo boasts over 125 native Belizean animals and is sprawled across 29 acres (12 hectares) of tropical savanna. These animals are either orphans, born at the zoo, rehabilitated, or gifts from other zoos. Welcoming more than 10,000 schoolchildren every year, the zoo also organizes popular events such as April the Tapir's birthday party, summer camps, a Science Fair, and teacher training and student career training programs. It is also the headquarters for the Tapir Specialist Group and maintains an active captive breeding program for the green iguana.

# LIFESTYLE

AS WITH ALL THINGS Belizean, there is a lot of diversity packed into a very small space. There is an endless variety of lifestyles, whether urban or rural; mainland or islander; rich or poor; male or female; Creole, Mayan, Garifuna, mestizo, Indian, or Mennonite.

## ISLANDERS

Islanders living on the cays have seen dramatic changes to their way of life in the last 20 years. The heavily populated cays such Ambergris and Caulker have become tourist meccas since the 1980s. Previously, people on the islands depended on fishing to make a living and were isolated from the mainland. They traded with Belize City to obtain lumber for house construction and food they could not grow themselves, but life was fairly

*Left:* **Fishermen from Cay Caulker socializing.**

*Opposite:* **Schoolboys having fun.**

independent of the hustle and bustle of the city. Cay dwellers were reliant on each other, and there was almost no crime as everyone knew everyone else.

The influx of tourists, however, has brought many changes to this tranquil existence. Changes have been more dramatic in San Pedro, on Ambergris Cay, than on Cay Caulker, but there are many similarities. For example, land prices have increased tremendously, and in some areas, Belizeans have been priced out of the market as Americans and other foreigners compete to buy beachfront property. The availability of regular transportation to the mainland means local residents can reach services in Belize City easily, but it also means that people come and go at such a rate that life has become more impersonal and crime goes unpunished. Crime has partly come with tourism because tourists bring habits such as drug use with them and often have expensive belongings that are a source of temptation. Some islanders have traded in their fishing nets for a tourist business like a small hotel, restaurant, or guide service. One benefit from tourism is that women can earn their own money and gain some independence. Belizean islanders have continued to adapt to ever changing economic and social circumstances.

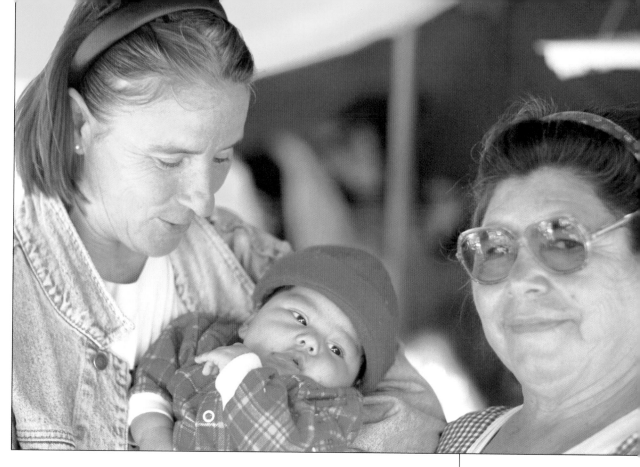

## FAMILIES AND CHILDREN

The family is very important to Belizeans of all backgrounds. Where the colonial and independent governments have been unwilling or unable to provide basic services for the population, people have relied on their close and extended families for work, childcare, healthcare, social assistance, and companionship. The form that the family takes differs from one community to another, but the idea of family and kinship is universal.

Among Creole Belizeans, there is a tendency to have matriarchal households. This is a pattern found across the Caribbean and stems from a history of slavery. In early colonial times male slaves often worked far from Belize City cutting lumber, while women worked as domestic help in the city. In modern times this migration for work has continued, with men migrating to the United States. For Belizean men who cannot afford to provide regular support or to pay for a church wedding ceremony, there are common-law marriages and "visiting" arrangements. A common-law marriage is one where the man and woman are not legally married but live

*Above:* **A Belizean woman with her mother and new-born baby.**

*Opposite:* **The manager of a tour agency in Belize City.**

It is often the women who look after the daily needs of the family. Here, the women are drawing water from a well.

together in a stable relationship. "Visiting" relationships are when the father of the children lives with his mother and siblings and only visits the mother of his children occasionally. He will contribute to the household when he has work. Creole women become the backbone of the family, as it is they who provide for children and help each other with childcare. Often children are raised by their grandmother if their mother is a single parent and has to work or migrates to the United States to find work.

For wealthier Belizeans, the norm is a nuclear or extended family. This means that husband and wife live with their children and sometimes their parents or siblings. Everyone contributes to the family unit. In rural communities women help with agricultural work and maintain the house, while men farm and sometimes work for wages. Older relatives provide childcare when necessary. Beyond the household is a wider network of relatives who can be relied on in times of need.

Family size differs across the cultural spectrum with recent mestizo migrants tending to have more children (3 to 4 on average per couple). In matriarchal households, the children born to one woman may not necessarily share one father. These children used to be discriminated against by society and viewed under the law as "illegitimate." Under colonial law, children born to parents who were not legally married were considered to have no rights to paternal support or to any part of their father's estate. Since many Belizeans are born to unwed parents, this posed a serious problem. In 1980 the law was changed to enforce support by the father. Children born out of wedlock are now considered to have the same rights to their parents' estate as legitimate children.

## WOMEN

Although the specific roles of women differ among the various ethnic groups, generally speaking, Belizean women do not have equal rights. While they may have certain rights in law, such as the right to vote, they do not earn the same wages for their work outside the home as men do, and are not paid and seldom recognized for their important contribution to family life. Since the 1980s, there have been more opportunities, particularly in urban areas, for women to find employment. Tourism has created a demand for small restaurants, hotels, and travel agencies where women can work or own their own businesses. Clothing assembly plants also rely exclusively on women's labor, although women do not have the right to a fair wage. In rural areas women have typically worked outside the home, whether on their family's farm or in small-scale trade, though it is mostly men who work on plantations for wages. Since the late 1970s, Belizean women have begun to organize themselves for change and for more protection under the law.

Three Mayan women run a produce stand at Corozal Town, which lies on the Mexican border.

An adult education class at Belize City.

## LEAVING BELIZE

The first wave of emigrants to the United States arrived as agricultural workers during the labor shortage of World War II. A small trickle of 2,000 turned into a flood in subsequent years. Official numbers recorded 55,000 to 60,000 Belizeans in the United States, concentrated in cities such as New York, Los Angeles, Houston, Chicago, New Orleans, and Miami. Though these are the official numbers, there are probably at least another 100,000 illegal Belizeans in the United States. Between 1980 and 1991, 41,000 legal immigrants entered the United States from Belize. The bulk of the migrants (75%) come from the Creole and Garifuna segments of the population. Creoles have an advantage because they speak English, and the Garifuna learn English rapidly and effectively. Since their initial entry as agricultural workers, Belizeans have turned away from rural work and moved mostly to cities in search of industrial and service sector employment. Given the high unemployment and limited opportunities at home, young Belizeans are hoping for something better abroad.

This drain of people from the already tiny population of Belize has had a number of effects on those left behind. Until recently, most Belizean migrants to the United States were the better-educated middle classes from Belize City and Dangriga. This has created a "brain drain" as the more promising young workers fail to return once they complete their education abroad. Migrants, however, are often the source of income for their families in Belize. Their remittances account for some 12–15% of the Belizean gross domestic product, up to 10% of its per capita income, and are a significant part of the household budget. Only a small percentage of remittances is sent through official channels. More arrive in the form of gifts. This has created a dual currency system in which people use both the Belizean and the US dollar in their daily transactions, supporting consumer spending in Belize.

The drain of English-speaking Creoles, coupled with the recent influx of Spanish-speaking mestizos from other parts of Central America, is changing the cultural and social balance of the country. New mestizo arrivals are overwhelmingly poor, uneducated, rural people who are choosing to live in the countryside in communities with other mestizos. Spanish has become the majority language, and these new immigrants will soon form a sizeable voting block. Remaining Creoles worry that this will threaten their dominant position in politics. The government has vacillated between welcoming new people to Belize to make up for labor shortages, particularly in export agriculture (sugar, citrus, and bananas), and restricting their entry because they are largely Spanish-speaking and poor.

Belizean currency. One hundred Belizean cents equals a Belizean dollar (Bz$).

The economic crisis of the 1990s affected the outward flow of Belizeans. Fewer Belizeans left as legal migrants to the United States; 60% entered or stayed in the United States illegally. Even fewer have maintained ties with their families at home, being younger and less well-educated and having to cope with higher costs of living in the United States. Those who return bring back American cultural influences. Unfortunately, some who have been deported from the United States because of illegal activities have also brought back violent behavior. Other returnees, however, are contributing to the development of Belize.

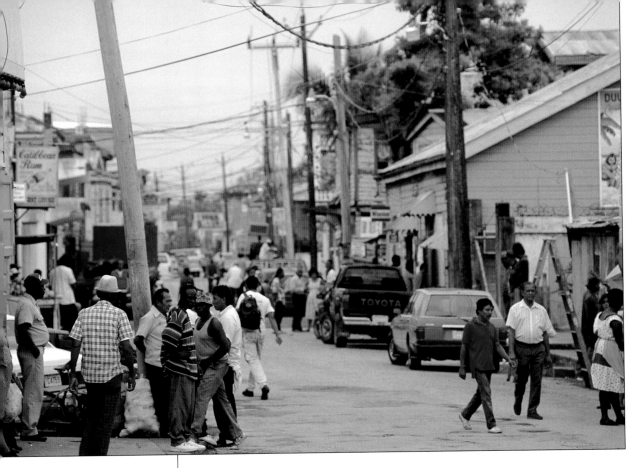

A street scene in Belize City.

## *RURAL VERSUS URBAN LIVING*

Like most developing countries, Belize experienced a trend toward urbanization. By 1970, 54% of Belizeans lived in urban centers. Since then, this trend has reversed; in 1991, 52.5% lived in rural areas. This pattern is not the same for all districts. Belize District, in particular, is very urbanized, with a fairly constant 80% of its population living in Belize City. The other districts, Cayo, Toledo, Stann Creek, Orange Walk, and Corozal, have always been more rural than urban. The trend toward urbanization slowed and then reversed through the 1970s and 1980s because of migration patterns. The thousands of Belizeans who left the country mainly came from urban areas; this was offset by the 40,000 mestizo newcomers who arrived after 1980 and settled in urban areas.

Rural dwellers in Belize do not have the same access to essential services and are much poorer than urban dwellers. On the other hand, urban dwellers face a higher crime rate and poor sanitation. One's class also determines the quality of one's urban life.

## EDUCATION

The literacy rate in Belize is 75%, which is high compared to other Central American countries. However, the existing educational system is badly in need of reform and expansion to handle the growing number of Spanish-speaking, poor, and rural students. Prime Minister Musa has committed 30% of his budget to meet some of these goals and is approaching private businesses for sponsorship.

A school in Corozol Town.

Belizean schools were started by religious orders who built schools alongside churches. The modern system is a combination of state and church-run schools. Elementary education is compulsory for children aged 6 to 14. However, in 1996 the mean number of years of education was only 7.7, meaning that many children are not completing even elementary school. Only about one third of young people attend secondary school and even fewer are able to attend post-secondary training colleges or universities. There are several reasons for this. In poor rural and urban areas parents often cannot afford schoolbooks or registration fees. Also, some children are too hungry to concentrate since they do not eat breakfast at home. Children from poor families, particularly boys, are often pressured to start work at a young age. There are also an insufficient number of qualified teachers in Belize.

Prime Minister Musa's government has drafted "The New Education Charter" to address some of these problems. The charter includes plans to build 1,000 new school rooms, train more teachers, establish a school canteen program for poor children, set up a textbook program, and introduce an improved curriculum for elementary schools.

Herbal medicine for sale at Belize City.

## *HEALTH*

Belize fares better than some of its neighbors such as Honduras in healthcare, but it still faces some serious health problems. Malaria continues to be a concern in rural Belize. The government has tried to eradicate the *Anopheles* mosquito that carries the malaria-causing organism, but it persists in rural jungle areas. Dengue fever, another mosquito-borne disease, is another health worry. Controlling malaria and dengue involves general hygiene in the form of garbage disposal as well as programs using insecticides. Many Belizeans have also died of AIDS (Acquired Immune Deficiency Syndrome) since the 1980s, and there were no facilities to test for HIV (Human Immunodeficiency Virus) until 1990. Belizeans, especially babies and children, are also vulnerable to diarrhea caused by unclean water and inadequate sanitation systems.

The majority of Belizeans have access to government hospitals, clinics, and maternal, childcare, and dental facilities. Infant mortality rates have been reduced by improved water supplies, waste disposal systems, disease control, and vaccination programs. However, most hospitals are sorely in need of upgrading, and there is a shortage of doctors and dentists, especially in the rural areas. This is because most doctors and dentists are foreigners, and only nurses are trained locally. A new social security program was created in the 1980s to provide pensions for senior citizens and to extend assistance to sick, disabled, pregnant, and unemployed workers and the families of deceased insured workers.

## *HOUSING*

There are a few main styles of house construction in Belize. One is the wooden clapboard style famous throughout the English-speaking Caribbean. These buildings can be seen along the coast and on the cays. Smaller houses may have only one or two indoor rooms with most cooking taking place outside. Larger wooden houses often have a covered veranda encircling the front and sides where people can relax and enjoy the sea breezes. Such houses usually do not have glass windows unless the owners are wealthy. Instead there are hinged shutters that can be closed against rain but still allow air circulation. In low-lying areas like Belize City, houses are often built on stilts so that they remain dry during the rainy season. In the rural inland areas whitewashed mud or wood and thatch houses are more common. Across the country, there has been a trend toward using concrete blocks and metal roofs as a substitute for older styles. Concrete needs less upkeep than wood, which is susceptible to termites and decay, or than wattle and daub houses that erode in the rain.

A wooden clapboard house near Belmopan.

Diocese of Belize

## "Hoy, No Manana."

# ST. JOHN'S CATHEDRAL

Foundation stone laid 1812 - Consecrated 1826
Anglican / Episcopal

## SUNDAYS

Holy Communion.................................................7:00 a.m.
Holy Communion / Family Service......................9:30 a.m.
Evening Prayers ...............................................6:00 p.m.
( 2nd Sunday, Holy Communion )
Baptismal: Every Second Sunday........................9:30 a.m.
Baptismal Interview: Friday Before.......................6:00 p.m.

## WEEKDAYS

Mondays, Major Feasts Day / Holy Communion....... 6:30 a.m.
Tuesdays, Holy Communion.................................... 9:00 a.m.
Wednesdays, Holy Communion...............................6:30 a.m.
Thursday, Holy Communion /
Memorials By Request........................................ 7:00 p.m.
Fridays, Holy Communion.................................... 6:30 a.m.
Saturdays, Major Feasts Days / Holy Communion....6:30 a.m.
Saturdays, Misa en Espanol................................. 6:00 p.m.

## BAPTISMAL, WEDDINGS, FUNERALS

By Appointment.

# RELIGION

THE MAJORITY OF BELIZEANS are Roman Catholics, followed by Anglicans and Methodists. The Mennonites, who are congregationalist Protestants, are the fourth-largest religious community in Belize. Fundamentalist and evangelical churches, many based in the United States, are growing rapidly in Belize. There are a few other religions and belief systems as well, including Islam, Hinduism, Judaism, and the Ba'hai faith. As in everything else, Belize's religions are a liberal mixture of traditions and peoples.

## *CHRISTIANITY*

The original Baymen were all Protestants so the first church to be established in the new territory was the Anglican Church of England,

*Left:* **St. Peter Claver Catholic Church in Punta Gorda.**

*Opposite:* **A signboard showing the services at St. John's Cathedral in Belize City.**

St. John's Cathedral in Belize City. It was rebuilt after being completely destroyed by a hurricane in 1931.

which was incorporated into the Jamaican diocese in 1824. At that time, Christianity and church attendance was exclusively a white affair. Back home in England, humanitarian church reformers were pressuring the Colonial Office to adopt policies to protect slaves from mistreatment. The reformers also conducted missionary work among the slaves in an effort to teach them English and introduce them to Christianity. But the Church of England prohibited its missionaries from acting against the wishes of the slave owners, and this prompted an antiestablishment evangelical movement among Anglicans and the rise of nonconformist churches like the Baptist Church and Wesleyan Methodist Church. Both churches sent missions to Belize in the 1820s. They gave the slaves basic education and helped them through the transition from slavery to freedom in 1838 when slavery was abolished in all British dominions. These two reform churches still operate today in Belize, though with a reduced following. There is still a stigma attached to membership in these denominations, and their members tend to be the poorer Belizeans.

Belize today is largely Roman Catholic. When the Yucatec and Mopan Mayas came from Mexico and when the Kekchí came from Guatemala, they brought Roman Catholicism with them. The vast numbers of Central American economic and political refugees that have come to Belize in the last 20 years have also been Roman Catholics. Many Garifuna are also Roman Catholic. The Catholic Church first arrived in the form of two Jesuit priests in 1851 and the first church was built in Corozal Town. In 1883 the Sisters of Mercy arrived to found a girls' school, St. Catherine's Academy, and a convent. Jesuits founded the prestigious St. John's College in 1887. Traditionally a private school for the upper classes, graduation from this school signaled that a boy was of the right background and ability to be a leader in business or politics. In modern Belize, St. John's still offers top quality education but has opened its doors to the wider population through a system of scholarships. It is also innovative in the arts and literature.

Other churches were established during colonial times, including a Scottish Presbyterian Church in 1851 and the American-based Seventh Day Adventists, who started a Belizean mission in 1891. Evangelical Christian churches from the United States have gained support in Belize. They began to send missions to Belize and other parts of Central and South America in the 1970s and 1980s. For a while in the early 1980s, evangelical bible study groups, corner churches, social programs, and schools appeared all over the country. The arrival of television, however, has slowed this growth in urban areas. In remote rural areas, especially the Mayan South, missionaries have been more successful in converting people, and there has been an increase in church schools and a decline in alcohol abuse.

Mount Zion Seventh Day Adventist Tabernacle in Belize City. The Seventh Day Adventists brought basic dental and medical care to coastal dwellers at the turn of the 20th century. They still operate charitable hospitals in Belize.

# MENNONITES

The Mennonite religion is a type of Protestant Christianity. Mennonites believe in following the New Testament of the Christian Bible, particularly the Sermon on the Mount. They believe that there should be a separation of church and state. So, for example, they refuse to have their children educated in state-run schools and prefer to run their own schools in German. As part of their commitment to the "simple life" promoted in the Bible, they reject fancy clothes and the use of machines. They believe in the supremacy and singularity of God and do not worship false idols. This means that they do not support such symbols as a national flag or anthem, do not hold public office, and refuse to pay state taxes. They are pacifists, which means that they reject any and all forms of violence and will not bear arms or go to war for their country.

All these beliefs and practices have made it difficult for Mennonites to live in peace, separated as they are from national life. Mennonite communities were often persecuted by other religions and the state, so in the 17th century many of them settled in other places, arriving for example in Pennsylvania in 1683, where they formed a group called the Pennsylvania Dutch. There was also a large exodus of Mennonites from Europe to Canada and Mexico following World War I. Then in the 1950s, fearing that the government was going to try to force them to join the social security system, many Mexican Mennonites left Mexico to settle in Belize.

## *RASTAFARIANISM*

Rastafarians worship Haile Selassie I, former emperor of Ethiopia. His precoronation name was Ras (Prince) Tafari. They consider him a divine being, the Messiah, and the champion of the black race. A core belief of Rastafarianism is the belief that black people are a reincarnation of the ancient Israelites and will one day return to Africa to establish a Black Zion under the leadership of a black king.

Rastafarianism is a politico-religious movement with its center in the highlands of Jamaica. Most Rastas outside Jamaica practice only a few of the principles of the religion. In Belize it is mostly young Creole men who are attracted to the Rasta look and lifestyle. They are often unemployed and depend on tourists to support them. Dogmatic Rastas abstain from liquor and red meat but believe that marijuana has spiritual properties. They are easily recognized by the fact that they do not cut their hair but tie it in braids called dreadlocks. It is a religion associated with popular reggae singer Bob Marley.

**Rastafarians at Caulker Cay.**

79

**Garifunas dancing at Seine Bight.**

## *GARIFUNA BELIEFS*

Although the Garifuna attend Roman Catholic and Methodist churches, they also maintain ancient beliefs and rituals, at times combining them with the formal practice of Catholicism. There are three main ancestral rites practiced by the Garifuna: the *amuyadahani* (Bathing the Spirit of the Dead); the *chugu* (Feeding of the Dead); and the *dugu* (Feasting of the Dead). *Dugu* ("DOO-goo") is the most sacred, elaborate, and best demonstration of Garifuna respect, appreciation for, and communion with their ancestors.

*Dugu* rites are performed on the request of a deceased ancestor, which is made known in a ceremony called *arairaguni* (bringing down) held by a *buyae* or medium. The *buyae* calls upon his *hiuruha* or spirit helper to explain a particular problem, such as an unexplained death in the family. The *buyae* and *hiuruha* communicate with the family's deceased ancestors, or *gubida,* to ascertain the cause of this death, which may be a form of punishment by an angered great grandfather. The *gubida* will then request a *dugu* as an appeasement. Preparations for this rite involve inviting relatives and friends from Belize and abroad, obtaining particular foods and beverages requested by that ancestor, and setting a date for the rite with the *buyae*, who will also inform other official performers including drummers, performers dressed in red, singers, and selected fishermen. There are four types of dance during the *dugu*: a semisacred song of the women, a song and dance of supplication, a dance of rejoicing, and a dance in circular formation. The participants may go into a trance and assume the characteristics of the *gubida* during the ceremony.

## FOLK BELIEFS AND LEGENDS

Belizean superstitions come from African influences in Creole and Garifuna cultures and from Mayan influence through mestizo culture. Some of these beliefs are found in other parts of Central America and the Caribbean. Some superstitions include the belief that seeing a certain species of black butterfly will cause an early death or bad luck, or that shoes should be crossed at night so that evil spirits will not occupy them, bringing the owner bad luck the next day. From Mayan tradition comes the belief that dreams are omens of the future. For example, a dream with red tomatoes in it means a baby will die.

In addition to folk beliefs, legends are popular among Belizeans. Local children learn about Belizean dwarves, known by their Spanish name *duendes* ("doo-EN-days"). *Duendes* are both evil and possess magical powers. If they capture you, they can make you go crazy, but they can also turn you into an expert musician on the instrument of your choice. They are said to live in the forest and if you see one, you should salute him, being careful to hide your thumb as they do not have thumbs and are jealous of those who do. They are said to be short and covered in thick dark hair. Some people claim that the ancient Maya portrayed *duendes* in their carvings.

Another forest dweller is the *sisimito* ("see-see-MEE-toh"), a hairy, man-like beast similar to the yeti of Asia and sasquatch of North America. *Sisimitos* have a reputation for killing men and stealing their women for mates. For a man to look into the *sisimito*'s eyes means death within a month. The *sisimito* wants desperately to learn how to make fire and to talk, and so may capture children to teach him language or sit for hours around an abandoned campfire watching the coals. There have been reports of *sisimitos* in Latin American for hundreds of years.

*Another folktale concerns a mysterious and ghostly pirate ship called the Jack O' Lantern that people claimed to have seen in the Stann Creek area. The boat is lit with flickering lanterns that are blamed for luring fishermen onto the coastal reef to their deaths.*

# LANGUAGE

ONE OF THE PRIMARY WAYS cultural difference is expressed in Belize is through language. Standard English is the official language of the country, but the majority of Belizeans speak localized versions of English or other languages at home and on the street.

## *CREOLE ENGLISH*

As a former colony of Great Britain, Belize retains Standard English as its official language. This is the language of instruction in government schools and for formal diplomatic and government business. It is not the most widely spoken form of English however. Creole English, a blend of different influences including Spanish and African languages, is the lingua franca of the country. To speakers of Standard English, whether British

*Left:* **A Belizean reading an English-language Belizean newspaper.**

*Opposite:* **Shop signs in English on Ambergris Cay.**

or American, creole English is only partly understandable. Some words are the same, but pronunciation and intonation are quite different. Belizean creole English shares many things in common with that of Jamaica, another former British colony. Since the beginning of the tourism boom in Belize, Americans and Canadians are also adding their style of English to the melting pot. With the arrival of television in the early 1980s, there has been even more American cultural influence.

## BELIZEAN SPANISH

Just as there are varieties of English spoken in Belize, there are also different types of Spanish spoken by Belizeans of different origins. The first mestizos who came from Mexico and Guatemala in the 19th century now speak what they call "kitchen Spanish," thus named to reflect its impure form. These Spanish-speakers have been exposed to English, as spoken by the British and Creoles, for so long that many English and Creole expressions and words have entered their Spanish. Some examples of Standard English words typically found in this type of Belizean Spanish are: shop, lunch, tip (as in gratuity), mile, holiday, creek, and pool. johnnycake (a type of bread or pancake), brain-law (brother-in-law), and John Canoe (Garifuna dance) are from creole English. In addition to English words, there are also changes in Spanish grammar in which the gender of a noun is switched or a verb is used differently. New strains of Spanish have entered the Belizean linguistic soup with new migrants from Guatemala, El Salvador, and Nicaragua. Their Spanish is less influenced by English expressions because the speakers come from monolingual Spanish countries.

*Opposite:* **Spanish-English shop signs.**

## OTHER LANGUAGES

English and Spanish are the dominant languages, but other languages are also spoken. Garifuna is spoken as the mother tongue of about 7% of the population. This is a language that combines features of Arawak and Carib with African languages. Garifuna is used in homes and areas like Dangriga where the majority of the population are Garifuna. In other parts of the

### CREOLE PROVERBS: CAN YOU FIGURE THEM OUT?

Creole English is quite similar to Standard English but is spoken with a different cadence and some words are different. Here are some examples of proverbs in creole and Standard English:

Creole English:
"Punkin never bear watermelon."
"Coward man keep sound bone."
"Fool dey talk, but dey no fool—dey lisson."

Standard English:
"Pumpkin plants don't produce watermelons."
"A coward doesn't get injured."
"Fools talk a lot but wise people listen."

country, Garifuna speak either creole English or Spanish. About 10% of Mayan peoples have also retained their languages. The Kekchí Maya of Toledo still learn Kekchí as their first language, although most are bilingual in Spanish. Northern Maya tend to speak Spanish as their mother tongue and have lost their Mayan language completely. Finally, the Belizean Mennonites speak German and teach their own children in this language. This German is quite distinct from modern European German. Its roots are from the German spoken about a century ago when the ancestors of this group originally left Europe. Most Mennonite men, and some of the women, also speak English and Spanish to communicate with their non-German-speaking neighbors.

**Kekchí Mayas at a market at Punta Gorda.**

## *LINGUISTIC CHANGES*

Apart from languages changing internally, there have also been significant changes in the overall linguistic landscape of Belize. Around 1950, 60% of Belizeans spoke English as their first language, 22% spoke Spanish, 10% spoke a Mayan dialect, and the remainder spoke Garifuna or another language. By 1980, English speakers dropped to 51% and Spanish speakers increased to 32%, although Mayan speakers held constant at 10%. By the turn of the 21st century, English speakers have dwindled to about 33%, while Spanish speakers have increased to 44%. Mayan speakers still account for 10%, German speakers 2%, and Garifuna speakers have dwindled to 7%. This shift, due in large part to migration, has resulted in the emergence of a new linguistic society in which bilingualism in Spanish and English is increasingly necessary.

## *VERBAL SKILLS*

Many writers on Belize comment on the importance of verbal interaction in daily life. This is not surprising if one considers the history of telecommunications in this tiny country. In the early 1970s the telephone system connected only 3,800 homes and businesses. This number increased to 8,600 in 1983, when all district capitals were finally connected. Cay Caulker had only one telephone for the whole island in 1982. With satellite and cellular technology, most middle-class Belizeans now own telephones. Previously, most interaction between individuals took place in face-to-face meetings. That meant that one's word was one's honor and a verbal agreement was enough to seal a deal. Hence, linguistic skills were

Belizeans relaxing and exchanging stories at a corner market in San Pedro, Ambergris Cay.

highly prized and cultivated. Telling a good story was a way to amuse and impress friends, even if the facts were stretched a little for entertainment value. Creole English is known for the colorful way ideas are expressed and considered to be superior to Standard English in this regard. With the arrival of modern telecommunications, including television, video, and telephone, face-to-face conversation and storytelling have given way to long-distance communication. Belizeans now are entertained by satellite programs and foreign movies.

## THE EARLY DAYS OF THE TELEPHONE

Author Anne Sutherland has lived in Belize for over 30 years. In her book *The Making of Belize*, she recounts a story of how Belizeans used telephones when they first came to Cay Caulker:

"Communication was strictly face-to-face. This may be why in Belize, when the telephone came in, it was common to have the following phone conversation:

(Ring) Hello.
Is Lindsay there?
Yes. (Click)
(Ring) Hello.
Hello, I asked if Lindsay was there.
Yes, I told you he is.
Well, may I speak with him?
Oh, sure. Why didn't you say so?

People assumed that the purpose of a phone call was to find out if someone else was there so the caller could come over and talk face-to-face. No one could expect to get anything done by speaking on the telephone."

# ARTS

BELIZEAN ARTS AND CRAFTS reflect the whole spectrum of cultural diversity. While Belize has had to struggle to produce its own artistic, literary, and musical traditions against the overwhelming influence of the British and now faces the challenge of American culture, there is ample evidence that Belizeans are creative and resilient enough to overcome the odds despite being a tiny country with limited resources.

## CULTURAL INFLUENCES

Being part Central American and part Caribbean, Belize enjoys cultural influences from many sources. It is also a country in transition so cultural traditions that once dominated the arts are now sharing space with new ideas. European influences are felt most strongly in language, where

*Left:* **A man playing the marimba.**

*Opposite:* **A Mayan woman showing off traditional handwoven textiles.**

English and Spanish dominate. Indigenous cultural traditions are apparent in the language and practices of the Kekchí Maya, Yucatec Maya, and Mopan Maya, as well as in the language of the Garifuna. African traditions, particularly in music, come through in both Creole and Garifuna rhythms and instruments. In the last 20 years the newest influence has been a global one: the cultural exports of the United States. This cultural element affects, to different degrees, every country and culture on the planet, but Belize is particularly susceptible because of its intimate social ties with the United States through the migration of its people. Top 40 music hits are frequently heard on Belizean radio, and clothing styles, particularly in urban centers, are influenced by American television and movies. Tourists, who are bearers of culture, also bring their habits and customs with them. This makes it extremely difficult to keep local traditions alive. However, American tourists are providing a small market for some Belizean artists and craftspeople who would otherwise not be able to make a living from their work.

# LITERARY ARTS

Under the British, Belizean literature was written exclusively in Standard English. Now there is a growing movement to write in creole English, the lingua franca of most Belizeans. The first Belizean novelist to gain recognition is Zee Edgell. Her first book was *Beka Lamb*, published in 1982. She has continued her critical success with second and third novels: *In Times Like These* (1991) and *The Festival of San Joaquin* (1997). Women are central characters in all three of her novels, which are set in Belize and grapple with problems the country faced during and after colonialism. *The Festival of San Joaquin* deals with environmental profiteering and the role of evangelical churches in modern Belize. *Beka Lamb* portrays a young Creole girl in Belize City in the 1950s and celebrates Belizean life by its unapologetic focus on everyday aspects of local family life, education, and the politics of the early independence movement. There has been a growing nationalism and pride in Creole culture and an eagerness to draw on African and European elements of Belizean heritage.

A Belizean reading the *Belize Review.*

Since the end of colonialism, new magazines and journals have sprung up, primarily in Belize City. Cubola Publications is a local publishing house that specializes in young Belizean writers of fiction and nonfiction. *Belizean Studies* is written by the Belizean Studies Association of St. John's College and provides an outlet for Belizean research and writing. *Belize Currents* and *Belize Review* are magazines designed to attract investors and tourists to the country. *Amandala* and *Brudown* are two outlets for political discussion; the former the most politically independent newspaper in Belize, and the latter an arts and politics magazine.

## VISUAL ARTS

The arts scene has flourished in Belize since the rise of the independence movement of the 1950s and 1960s. In its early stages, the Belizean art scene was scattered and disorganized, and there were no formal means by which the government or schools could support the development of artists. Some pioneers, such as Philip Lewis, formed the group Soul to Art in 1974 to promote painters, sculptors, and printers through organized exhibits; more than 50 were held in Belize and Jamaica. More recently, St. John's College has started to offer an art program, and it is already bearing fruit. Before this program, aspiring artists either had to teach themselves or leave the country for formal training. As with doctors, many who were educated abroad chose not to return. Today, the relaxed pace of life and the opportunity to sell their works to tourists make Belize a new artists' haven.

*Philip Lewis specializes in pen and ink drawings of his Cay Caulker home. His drawings are simple and uncomplicated and capture snapshots of daily life.*

**A slate carving by the Garcia sisters in San Antonio, Cayo District. They take slate from local riverbeds and carve it into two or three-dimensional representations of animals, mythical figures from Mayan tradition, or portraits of daily life.**

## MUSIC

Belize shares many of its musical styles with Central America and the English-speaking Caribbean. One exception to this is a style called punta rock that originated among Belizean Garifuna people. Punta rock is based on traditional Garifuna dance and song patterns. The punta dance was often performed at wakes. The music is provided by drummers and people clapping their hands and chanting. A couple move around the dance floor using quick sideways shuffling steps and hip movements. Women can also dance the punta alone. The dance is accompanied by a type of call and response song in which local characters are derided or criticized without being named. In the early 1990s a modern form of punta developed among pop bands and became quite popular in Belize and Honduras. The new punta combined Garifuna rhythms and song styles with Calypso and reggae styles. Punta rock unites Garifuna and Creole musical traditions. Some of the Garifuna musicians who developed this style are Andy Palacio, Pen Cayetano, and Mohobob Flores.

**A Garifuna dance and drum group.**

A Creole style that has lost ground to modern international music is the calypso-like breakdown. Breakdowns have much in common with Garifuna punta because they too use songs to criticize local personalities or relate humorous incidents. In the 1940s steel bands performed in Belize City at Christmas time, and singers like William Trapp and Roderick Brown improvised breakdowns about that year's events or some notable British personality. These songs would then be popular all year long until the next round of breakdowns were invented. Today's breakdowns may not

**Creole turtle-shell drums.**

compete with modern Top 40 hits, but Christmas continues to be a time of spontaneous musical celebrations of singing and drumming called brams.

The Garifuna and Creoles are renowned drummers, and they have developed Belizean forms of drums from local materials. Typical Garifuna drum performances involve three drums of various sizes made from cedar wood and turtle shells. Garifuna and Creole drumming can be heard during a spontaneous party or local festival. The idea of drums was imported with the African slaves. Drums are central to African music and were used in Africa as a mode of communication between villages and as an essential element in religious performances. Slave owners tried to suppress drumming and dancing, but it survived despite their best efforts. Slaves would hold *gombays* ("GOM-bays"), or drumming and dancing parties, during which different African tribes would compete in dancing and drumming. *Gombay* also refers to a type of Belizean drum made from goatskin and played with the hand.

Although not exclusively Belizean, the marimba ("mah-REEM-bah") is an integral part of the musical culture of Belize. This percussion instrument is often played by the Maya and mestizos during festivities and celebrations. It is a type of xylophone with a wooden resonator. The resonator is the part of the instrument that amplifies the sound of the wooden crossbars being struck by mallets. Despite its popularity among the modern Maya, it is not a traditional Mayan instrument. The marimba came to the New World with African slaves but was later adopted by indigenous and mestizo peoples. Mestizo and Mayan peoples have also adopted instruments from the Spanish tradition such as guitars and violins.

# CRAFTS

Most tourists want something to take home as a reminder of their visit to Belize, and Belizean craftspeople are more than happy to comply. Some traditional crafts have been revived or maintained for this purpose, and many new ones have been developed.

Mayan weavers, using natural plant fibers, produce beautiful and useful objects such as bags, baskets, and hammocks. These items are still used by the people themselves but sales also bring in much needed money to households. Carving used to be a highly developed skill among the ancient Maya, but modern Mayan people no longer build and carve the beautiful stone temples of the past. Today, however, carving is revived for the tourist industry and for export. Popular materials include the nut of the cohune palm, coconut shell, and slate.

Ceramics are made all over the country and feature motifs from nature and Mayan art. Musical instruments are also made for sale, particularly Garifuna and Creole drums. Creole and Garifuna women produce handmade dolls. These dolls tend to be adult black women either dressed in their finest clothes or performing a domestic task. Mennonites make wooden furniture that is simple, functional, beautiful, and much sought after by locals and tourists.

A traditional Mayan skill is healing. Healers are knowledgeable about herbs and other plants that can cure or alleviate common ailments. That knowledge is now being used to develop herbal medicines and remedies for sale to Belizeans and foreigners.

**A Belizean handmade doll.**

BELIZE IS IN MANY WAYS quite similar to developed countries in its leisure activities and pastimes. However, leisure is a recent phenomenon in everyday Belizean life.

## THE HISTORY OF LEISURE IN BELIZE

As a logging camp, Belize Town offered little in the way of entertainment. Loggers worked hard in the forests cutting timber and returned to town to sell their wood to merchant ships. When the ships arrived at port, they announced their arrival with a canon shot. The most popular trade item was rum, brought from other West Indian sugar colonies. The loggers would squander their earnings on board these ships in drink and revelry. As the colony became more settled, an annual festival was held at

*Left:* **A bar in the Cayo District.**

*Opposite:* **Windsurfing near Cay Caulker.**

A church gathering was the only legal social gathering until 1945 as churches were the only institutions granted licenses for public entertainment.

Christmas. At this time, merchants would come to Belize to set up stalls to sell rum and food, and the loggers would party with abandon. As the British gained more control in the early 19th century, the Christmas tradition changed. British commanders would muster all able-bodied men into the Citizen's Militia for the week leading up to Christmas. Businesses were shut as their owners did their annual military training. There were balls and amusements but not the wild revelry of past times. This tradition lasted until the repeal of the Militia Law in 1846.

Missionaries of the Protestant Wesleyans finally brought the wild celebrations to an end, arguing instead for abstinence and sobriety. This lasted well into the 20th century. As late as 1945 the only social gatherings sanctioned by law were those focused on the church. There was no separate theater or nightlife in the form of dance clubs or bars. Private parties were supervised by the police. Of course, the situation has changed dramatically. Today there are bars, clubs, and dancehalls in larger towns, and people are no longer required to register their private parties. Fun has come a long way in Belize!

## PRE-TELEVISION ENTERTAINMENT

Television came to Belize fairly recently. Before the days of television and more recently, the primary social activity was talking with neighbors and friends. Men, in particular, would meet in public places after the day's work to discuss life. Every village has a canteen or local store that sells drinks where people can gather to chat. Women meet in other places such as at church events or along the street. In small towns and villages gossip is not only highly entertaining but also an integral part of social life. Gossip is a form of information exchange and keeps people abreast of developments among their neighbors. It also solidifies social groups by creating a group history. Those who gossip together affirm that they have a longstanding relationship. There were also organized church events. In addition to Sunday service, there would occasionally be dances or picnics.

Men playing checkers, one of the most popular games in Belize.

101

Birth, marriage, and death also provided entertainment. It may seem odd to talk about celebrating death, but among Creoles and Garifuna, there is an element of fun to a funeral, since everyone participates in it. At events such as weddings and funerals, storytelling and music are essential elements. Stories and folktales often contain a little history and information about cultural values and beliefs. Listening to the stories of the elders is one way for children to learn about their culture and for adults to reaffirm their beliefs. Music and dance are also part of entertainment in Belize.

## *RADIO AND TELEVISION*

The first radio broadcasts around Belize City took place in 1937. Those who could afford them bought radios and always made allowance in the family budget for batteries. There was even a fad for country and Western music in the 1940s because Belizean radio could pick up Texas stations. In 1952 Radio Belize opened its doors as the only legal national radio station.

Before telephones and television sets were available, the radio was everyone's main source of information about the world, the country, and each other, as Radio Belize used to devote a segment of its show to delivering personal messages. In this way, Belizeans away from home could learn about a sick relative or other emergencies. Listening to the evening broadcast everyday was a focal point of people's lives. Apart from news and weather, the radio also brought a variety of music styles to people in different parts of the country. Radio Belize always devoted up to a third of its airtime to Spanish-language broadcasts and music from Mexico and other Spanish-speaking countries in the region. It is estimated that 98% of Belizeans have access to a radio, and 95% listen to an expanded Radio Belize that now reaches every part of the country in AM and FM,

24 hours a day. There is competition from private radio stations. In 1990 Radio KREM began broadcasting from Belize City. It promotes local musical talent and black consciousness. Another small station in Cayo has been instrumental in organizing the local population to demand services from the government and features music.

There was no Belizean television station before the 1970s as the population was too small to warrant one. In 1978 an American entrepreneur sent video movies to ten Belizeans for rental to others and started a craze for television sets and videocassette recorders. It was not long before enterprising Belizeans built receivers to pirate television signals from Mexico and the United States. At first, in 1981 these signals were only available to those who could pay the fee charged by the owners of the receivers, but other Belizeans soon learned to pirate from the pirates and now television is widely available. Belize has a similar per capita (per person) rate of television ownership to that of the United States. There are now two Belizean stations, and the Belize Channel (Channel 5) is the most popular. It broadcasts programs on cultural events and has produced a number of excellent documentaries on current affairs and Belizean history. In the early days, television served as a focal point of social activity, with people gathering in restaurants or homes where there were sets. Now, as most people have their own set, television actually reduces the amount of time people spend socializing. The most popular programs in Belize are Mexican and American soap operas, movies, and Belizean variety shows.

**A man listening to the radio on a street in San Pedro.**

## INTERNET

Electronic mail and Internet access became available in 1995 through the work of a Canadian student who was working as a volunteer. Now there are a number of websites available both for Belizeans and to advertise Belize to the outside world. Belize Telecommunications Ltd. provides Internet access to local residents. Although the local Internet Service Provider had only listed 550 electronic mail addresses as of 1998, as with television and telephone, this technology will soon proliferate. If television has opened Belize to influences from its two giant North American neighbors (Mexico and the United States), then the Internet will open it to the world.

**The telephone exchange at San Pedro.**

## *SPORTS, GAMES, AND FADS*

The most popular local team sport is soccer. It became popular in England near the end of the 19th century and spread to Belize from there. Racing is also very popular. In addition, there are annual bicycle races, sailing races, and horse races. Most Belizeans live near water and enjoy swimming as a pastime. Among the games favored by Belizeans are bingo and checkers. Gambling, both legal and illegal, is also popular. Legal gambling includes such institutions as the National Lottery or Boledo ("boh-LAY-doh"), and slot machines are turning up in tourist resorts. There is some discussion about whether Belize will open its doors to casinos in the future. Many people oppose this on moral grounds but appreciate that it is a primary attraction for some tourists. Clubs and discos are frequented by young Belizeans who follow local, Caribbean, and North American music and dance fads. One trend that has caught on is nature conservation and appreciation. Belizeans have become aware of the natural beauty around them and are working hard to preserve it.

# FESTIVALS

FOR SUCH A SMALL COUNTRY, Belize has many festivals and holidays. Some mark special days in Belizean national history, while others are celebrated by specific cultural groups.

## CIVIC HOLIDAYS

These are holidays that do not have a religious basis such as Christmas or Easter. In Belize, Labor Day is celebrated on May 1. The Minister of Labor usually gives a public address at this time, and there are parades of workers and rallies around the country. There are also kite contests, bicycle races, regattas, and horse races. Another civic holiday is Independence Day on September 21. This is the formal date of independence from the British in 1981. Since St. George's Cay Day on September 10 is also a holiday

*Left:* **Dancers celebrating the Cashew Festival.**

*Opposite:* **A Garifuna drummer.**

commemorating Belizean history and national pride, the whole month of September tends to become a time of celebration. Independence is marked with flag-raising ceremonies, parades, and street celebrations. Other civic holidays include Garifuna Settlement Day and Columbus Day.

## AGRICULTURAL FAIRS & SPORTS EVENTS

There are a number of fairs held each year to mark Belize's progress in agriculture. The annual Agriculture and Trade Show is held in Belmopan and Orange Walk in March. Livestock and produce are exhibited, and there are dance performances and displays of local handicrafts. On the last weekend in March, there is a trade and livestock show featuring a small rodeo. Local sports are also featured throughout the year beginning with the International Billfish Tournament in February. The Belize Game Fish

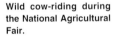
Wild cow-riding during the National Agricultural Fair.

Association sponsors this competition among fishermen to land a marlin weighing over 500 pounds (227 kg). There is prize money of some $50,000! Commonwealth Day on May 24 is also marked by sports events. This day is celebrated in many former British colonies as the Queen's birthday. On this day, there are horse races in Belize City and Orange Walk and cycle races between Cayo and Belmopan. Columbus Day celebrates indigenous cultures in the New World with sailing races or regattas in the harbor.

## LOCAL FAIRS

While some celebrations are nationwide, others are confined to particular villages and towns and reflect local pride and customs. In the Maya community of San Jose Succotz, the day of the patron saint—San Jose or Saint

A coconut toss competition during the Coconut Festival.

Joseph—is celebrated in April. There is plenty of entertainment including rides, food, and live marimba music. San Ignacio celebrates its food and crafts in the Cayo Expo every May. Also in May is the Coconut Festival on Cay Caulker. Local residents design and build floats to compete in a parade, and dance and enjoy a community party. The Toledo Festival of Arts is a week-long celebration in May when schoolchildren create plays that highlight the region's cultural diversity. Arts and crafts such as baskets, painting, and clay sculpture are exhibited. In June San Pedro celebrates its patron saint and that of fishermen, Saint Peter. This is a three-day event. Part of the festivities include a boat parade, the blessing of boats and fishermen, and a special Catholic mass. The mestizos of Orange Walk and Corozal participate in Mexico's National Day in September.

Carnaval dancers in
Belize City.

## *CARNAVAL*

As in many other Latin American countries where there are Roman
Catholics, carnaval (Spanish for "carnival") is celebrated among Spanish-
speakers on Ambergris Cay. Carnaval is celebrated sometime in February
or March, a few days before the beginning of Lent. Lent is a period of
abstinence for Catholics, when they give up eating meat and other favorite
foods and beverages. Since Lent is supposed to be a somber time to reflect
on the crucifixion of Christ at Easter, the traditional European custom was
to have a wild party beforehand. In San Pedro carnaval is celebrated with
games in which people throw flour and talc on one another and paint each
other with lipstick or paint. Carnaval is becoming more organized, with
competing groups of musicians and dancers, similar to the famous ones
in Brazil and Trinidad and Tobago.

## BARON BLISS DAY

Henry Edward Ernest Victor Bliss was the fourth Baron Bliss of the former Kingdom of Portugal. He was born and raised in England and first came to Belize in 1926 on his yacht, the *Sea King*. Due to illness, he never left the ship but spent several months anchored in the harbor enjoying the climate and hospitality of Belize. He died in Belize and was buried there. He was so grateful for the kindness and respect shown him by Belizeans that he left nearly $2 million as a trust fund for Belize. This money has been used to build clinics, water systems, and libraries. A portion of the fund is also used to host a yacht regatta every March 9, when Belize honors the Baron's contributions. In addition to boat races, there are also horse and bicycle races around the country.

## EASTER

As Belize is almost entirely Christian, there is an official four-day national holiday around Easter. Celebrations differ for different Christian denominations. For example, on Ambergris Cay and Cay Caulker where most of the inhabitants are Roman Catholic, there are special church services on Good Friday and processions carrying the cross through town. On Holy Saturday the Cross Country Classic is held between Belize City and San Ignacio. Cyclists from Belize and abroad participate in a race along the Western Highway as far as San Ignacio and back to the grand finale in Belize City. Easter Sunday and Monday are marked by family get-togethers, meals, and church ceremonies.

The Baron Bliss lighthouse and tomb in Belize City.

111

## THE CASHEW FESTIVAL

The Cashew Festival is held in Crooked Tree in northern Belize District on the first weekend of May to celebrate the cashew harvest. Cashew trees are native to this area, and their nuts are used in wine and jam and are sold both roasted and raw. This festival is celebrated with storytelling, arts, crafts, music, dancing, feasts, folkloric performances, and Carribean-style dishes, with an emphasis on cashew creations such as cashew jellies and wine. There are also demonstrations of cashew harvesting. This festival was actually started by a tour company based in the United States, but has become a celebration of Belizean culture and the preservation of the natural environment.

Part of the Cashew Festival celebrations includes the selection of a Cashew Queen by the residents of Crooked Tree.

# NATIONAL DAY

Belize's National Day celebrates the Battle of St. George's Cay, which took place in 1798 in the waters around St. George's Cay near Belize City. It began on September 3, when 31 Spanish ships carrying 2,000 soldiers and 500 sailors converged on the mouth of the Belize River to attack the combined British and Baymen force, which was only 350! There was a British warship, the *Merlin*, with 50 men and five local boats, *Towser*, *Tickler*, *Mermaid*, *Swinger*, and *Teaser*, each with 25 Baymen volunteers, and a number of small craft and rafts.

For the first few days, the Spanish tried to maneuver their ships so they could land their troops and establish a base on St. George's Cay. Since the Baymen and the British knew the local waters much better than the Spanish and had smaller, more manageable boats, they could position themselves to block the Spanish at every turn. Finally, the Spanish sent 14 rafts full of soldiers from their ships. Despite being greatly outnumbered, the British and Baymen valiantly fought off the attack. While the Spanish galleons were sitting immobile offshore, the British warship began to bombard them mercilessly. This attack lasted two and half hours before the Spaniards decided to cut anchor and run. Many Spaniards died in this failed attack. Miraculously, not one Bayman or British soldier was killed.

The battle did not change the status of Belize, which at that time was still not a formal British possession, but it was a source of local pride for the Baymen and has continued to represent Belize's national spirit of being small but strong. This spirit is celebrated around the country during the days leading up to National Day with parades, official ceremonies, pop music concerts, sporting activities, and a special parade of fire engines.

*In different parts of the country, there are festivals that are not celebrated as official holidays. These include carnaval and the International Billfish Tournament in February; the Agricultural and Trade Show in March; and the Mayan Deer Dance Festival in August.*

## *GARIFUNA SETTLEMENT DAY*

The first large group of Garifuna arrived in Belize on November 19, 1832 to settle in Stann Creek. There were a few Garifuna living there before then, but their presence was not significant. The week leading up to this day is busy with street dancing, drumming, and parties. Garifuna from all over the Caribbean region come to Belize for this important celebration of their culture. The festivities include a reenactment of the landing of Alejo Beni in 1832. There is also a religious ceremony, performed in the Garifuna language in the Catholic Church, that combines elements of Catholicism with African and Carib rituals. On that day, the main road in Dangriga is closed to traffic.

**The Garifuna like to reenact the journey of their forefathers as part of the festivities during Garifuna Settlement Day.**

## A CALENDAR OF OFFICIAL HOLIDAYS

| | |
|---|---|
| January 1 | New Year's Day |
| March 9 | Baron Bliss Day |
| March/April | Good Friday/Holy Saturday/Easter Sunday/Easter Monday |
| May 1 | Labor Day |
| May 24 | Commonwealth Day |
| September 10 | National Day, also called St. George's Cay Day |
| September 21 | Independence Day |
| October 12 | Columbus Day |
| November 19 | Garifuna Settlement Day |
| December 25 | Christmas Day |
| December 26 | Boxing Day |

## CARIBBEAN CHRISTMAS

In the weeks leading up to Christmas, Garifuna perform the John Canoe Dance on the streets of Punta Gorda, Dangriga, and Belize City. This is a dance with specific roles for the male dancers. There is a "king," "clown," and several boys dressed as pregnant women. Drummers and female singers accompany the dancers, who wear masks with mustaches, costumes, and decorative headdresses in mimicry of the finery of the colonial European masters. The dancers move from house to house in Dangriga, Belize City, and other Garifuna settlements, dancing for gifts of candy, rum, and money. The main dancer, the "king," mimics the arrogant walk of a European slave-owner to make people laugh. John Canoe used to be performed in other parts of the Afro-Caribbean such as Jamaica, but it seems to be dying out now. It has become pure entertainment in Belize, retaining elements that resemble a ritualized rebellion against colonial authority.

*Another Belizean festival is the Deer Dance festival, celebrated widely among Mayans. For the period of the festival, the whole village eats and drinks together. Dressed as deer, dancers perform the deer dance daily, moving from house to house. On the last day, a special pole, called the "money tree," is brought to the center of the village. Villagers try to climb its greased trunk to get the prize of money and rum attached at the top.*

# FOOD

BELIZE IS A PARADOX when it comes to food. There is a huge variety of food available from the land and the sea, but most Belizeans are contented to eat a fairly monotonous diet. As with lifestyle, there is no single standard; different ethnic groups and regions tend to favor different kinds of food.

## BASIC FOOD

For most Belizeans, meals are usually accompanied by, or consist entirely of, beans and rice. Beans are red or black and usually cooked in large batches with some sort of salted meat such as bacon for flavoring. Rice is the staple starch in the diet and is generally boiled. On special occasions rice will be cooked with coconut milk for added flavor and richness. Mayan

*Left:* **Beans and rice are Belizean staple foods.**

*Opposite:* **A vegetable market in San Pedro.**

**A man making tortillas.**

people, particularly in the South, substitute corn for rice as their staple. They grow the corn themselves and use corn flour to make the soft tortillas that accompany most meals. Nearer the coast, people eat more seafood, while those living inland depend more on chicken for protein. The Garifuna eat fish regularly, and on special occasions, will cook it in coconut milk for flavor. Coconut milk is a standard ingredient in Caribbean cooking. A typical Creole Sunday meal is coconut rice, beans, and chicken with gravy.

Bread, either leavened or unleavened "quick" bread, is also part of the regular Belizean diet. Some quick breads are made from wheat flour, others from corn. For example, the southern Maya grow corn and use the flour to make soft flat tortillas for everyday meals. On special occasions the Maya will make tamales that are made with corn meal, meat, and vegetables wrapped together in a banana leaf, then boiled. Another quick bread, called *bammie* ("bah-mee"), is made with cassava starch. Making cassava bread is a two-day process. The cassava tubers have to be dug up, then peeled and grated into a pulp. Liquid is forced manually out of this pulp down a tube strainer, releasing the flour into chunks into another pan. These chunks of flour are then flipped and baked over a fire to make cassava bread. Breadfruit and bananas can also be dried and ground into flour for making bread. Leavened breads are made with wheat flour and require yeast to make them rise. Wheat flour is used to make cakes, johnnycakes, jacks, and fritters. Johnnycakes are a type of sweet pancake, while jacks are a puff pastry. Both are eaten for breakfast with fruit preserves.

## CONCH *ESCABECHE*

Conch *escabeche* ("kahnk ES-kah-BAY-chay") or ceviche is a way of cooking fish without using heat. Lime or lemon juice is used to marinate the meat.

1 cup of conch or scallop meat
1 large ripe tomato, cut into one-inch (2.5 cm) cubes
1 large cucumber, cut into one-inch (2.5 cm) cubes
1 green pepper, diced
1/3 large yellow or white onion, diced
1 clove garlic, minced
1 large handful of fresh cilantro
1–2 limes
Salt & pepper to taste

Cut the seafood into one-inch cubes. Squeeze lime juice over it and let it stand. Add tomato, cucumber, green pepper, and onions. Mince garlic and chop the cilantro. Mix everything together and serve with tortilla chips and hot sauce.

## *VARIETY*

Although Belizeans may have a fairly monotonous diet, it is also true that there are foods and methods of preparation available that are fantastic in their variety. The forests contain all sorts of wild game available to hunters. For example, the gibnut or paca, a rabbit-like rodent, was served to Queen Elizabeth on her formal visit some years ago. There are wild ducks, iguanas and iguana eggs, deer, armadillo, and peccary. The southern Maya cook wild game in spicy sauces.

The sea and rivers provide their own bounty. Along the coast and in the cays can be found conch, shark, sea turtle, lobster, squid, red snapper, shrimp, sea bass, and barracuda. Although sea turtles are an endangered species, Belizean law allows hunting at certain times of the year. Conch is one of nature's most versatile foods and is delicious. For seafood lovers who cannot decide which fish or shellfish they prefer, there is "boil up." This is a stew made from whatever could be caught that day, cooked with coconut milk and spices. Sweet potatoes, tomatoes, peppers, squash, pumpkin, and avocados are all native to Central America. Mangoes, guava, pawpaws, bananas, plantain, grapefruit, and breadfruit also grow here.

## SEASONING

Belizeans know how to use spices and herbs to add flavor to any dish. Their repertoire of seasonings is drawn from diverse traditions and cuisines. Among the more familiar seasonings are basil, bay leaf, dill, garlic, ginger, marjoram, mint, oregano, sage, thyme, and parsley. Others are more exotic, such as cilantro, and achiote or anato (a fruit boiled to form a paste used in cooking). East Indians have introduced curry to Belize. Mayan and Mexican traditions have contributed two other mixed seasonings in the form of pastes: red recardo and black recardo. The red version uses anato, garlic, black pepper, onion, and vinegar that is packed into balls and used in tamales and meat dishes. Black recardo combines burned corn tortillas, onion, garlic, cloves, black pepper, and vinegar and is used with bean fillings. The Garifuna use seaweed to flavor certain dishes.

Belizeans use a variety of hot peppers to add zing to their food. The most common is the habanero pepper. Belize is home to a famous hot sauce—Marie Sharp's. Marie Sharp's Fine Foods Ltd. began operation in 1982 and is a small family-run business in the foothills of the Maya Mountains in the district of Stann Creek. The company buys fruit and vegetables from local growers to support small-scale agriculture in the region. It also produces jam, spreads, and other sauces. The hot sauce contains habanero peppers, carrots, onions, lime juice, vinegar, garlic, and spices. It can be found on most Belizean tables and it can now be purchased in the United States.

**Marie Sharp's fiery hot habanero sauce.**

## BEVERAGES

As with many tropical countries, the most refreshing drinks are made with fresh fruit. Almost any fruit can be combined with water or ice to make a delicious drink. Belize also produces its own soft drinks that are widely available, in addition to well-known foreign brands. Belikin beer is the local brand and Belizeans are quite proud of it. Rum is also produced from sugarcane. The Garifuna have a couple of alternative alcoholic drinks such as cashew wine and "local dynamite," a combination of rum and coconut milk. For a nonalcoholic energy drink, there is chicory-flavored coffee. Mint is added to hot water to make a refreshing tea.

The local Belikin beer is drunk with most meals.

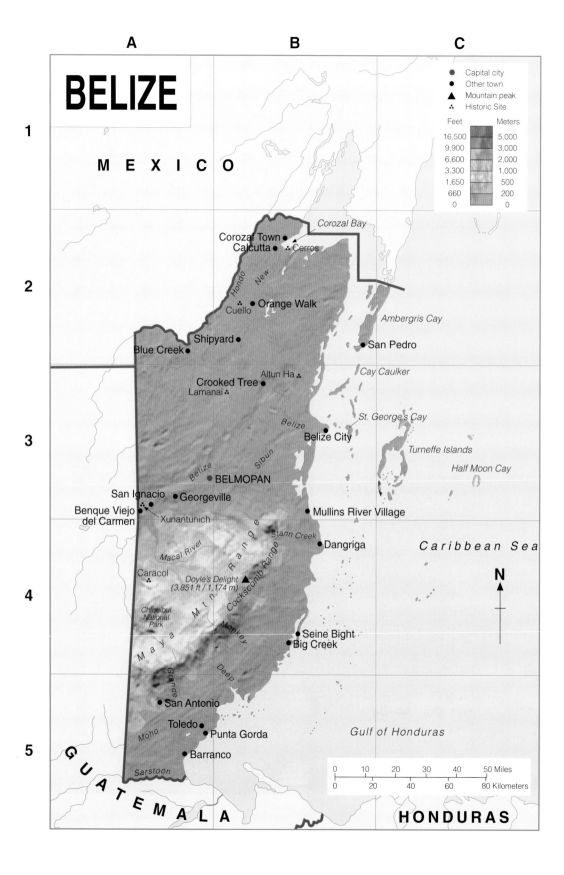

# BELIZE

A     B     C

1

M E X I C O

Corozal Bay

Corozal Town ●
Calcutta ● ⋅⋅⋅ ● Cerros

Hondo
New

2

Cuello ⋅⋅⋅ ● Orange Walk

Ambergris Cay

Shipyard ●
Blue Creek ●
● San Pedro

Altun Ha ⋅⋅⋅
Crooked Tree ●
Lamanai ⋅⋅⋅

Cay Caulker

Belize

St. George's Cay

3

Belize City ●

Turneffe Islands

Half Moon Cay

Sibun

Belize

● BELMOPAN

San Ignacio ●
● Georgeville

Benque Viejo ⋅⋅⋅
del Carmen   Xunantunich

● Mullins River Village

Macal River

Stann Creek

Caribbean Sea

● Dangriga

Caracol ⋅⋅⋅

Doyle's Delight ▲
(3,851 ft / 1,174 m)

Chiquibul
National
Park

Cockscomb Range

Mtn.

Monkey

N

4

M a y a

Range

● Seine Bight
Big Creek ●

Grande

Deep

● San Antonio

Toledo ●
● Punta Gorda

Moho

Gulf of Honduras

5

● Barranco

Sarstoon

G U A T E M A L A

HONDURAS

### Legend

● Capital city
● Other town
▲ Mountain peak
⋅⋅⋅ Historic Site

| Feet | Meters |
|------|--------|
| 16,500 | 5,000 |
| 9,900 | 3,000 |
| 6,600 | 2,000 |
| 3,300 | 1,000 |
| 1,650 | 500 |
| 660 | 200 |
| 0 | 0 |

0   10   20   30   40   50 Miles
0   20   40   60   80 Kilometers

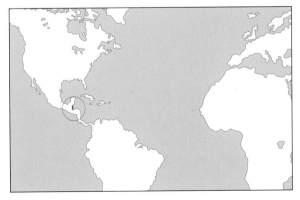

# QUICK NOTES

**OFFICIAL NAME**
Belize

**CAPITAL**
Belmopan

**LAND AREA**
8,867 square miles (22,965 square km)

**CLIMATE**
Subtropical climate, high rainfall and humidity. Average temperature is 79°F (26°C). Annual mean temperature in Belize City: 74°F (23°C) in December and 84°F (27°C) in July.

**HIGHEST POINT**
Doyle's Delight (3,851 feet or 1,174 m)

**MAJOR RIVERS**
Belize, New, Hondo, Sibun, Monkey, Deep, Grande, Moho, Sarstoon

**CAYS**
Ambergris, Caulker, St. George's, Half Moon, Turneffe Islands

**POPULATION**
249,200 (2000 estimate)

**MAJOR TOWNS**
Belize City, Orange Walk, San Ignacio, Corozal Town, Dandriga

**NATIONAL PLANT AND ANIMAL**
Mahogany tree and Baird's tapir

**FLAG**
Dark blue with a narrow red stripe along the top and bottom edges. In the center is a large white disk with the coat of arms encircled with a green garland.

**ADMINISTRATIVE REGIONS**
Belize, Cayo, Corozal, Orange Walk, Stann Creek, Toledo

**LANGUAGES**
English (official), Spanish, creole English, Mayan, German, Garifuna

**MAJOR RELIGION**
Christianity. The majority are Roman Catholics, followed by Anglicans and Methodists.

**CURRENCY**
The Belizean dollar, 1 dollar = 100 cents. US$1=Bz$2

**MAIN IMPORTS**
Machinery and transportation equipment, food, manufactured goods, fuels, chemicals and pharmaceuticals

**MAIN EXPORTS**
Sugar, citrus fruits, bananas, clothing, fish products, molasses, wood

**MAJOR FESTIVALS**
Independence Day, National Day, Garifuna Settlement Day, Easter, Christmas, Cashew Festival, Coconut Festival, carnaval

# GLOSSARY

**achiote** ("ah-chee-OH-tay")
A fruit used to form a paste for flavoring food. Also called *anato* ("ah-NAH-toh").

**bammie** ("bah-mee")
A type of bread made with cassava starch.

**boil up**
A stew made with a variety of fish cooked in spices and coconut milk.

**Boledo** ("boh-LAY-doh")
The national lottery of Belize.

**bram**
A spontaneous musical celebration of singing and drumming.

**breakdown**
A type of music performed at Christmas with calypso bands in which the words criticize and make fun of local figures.

**cay** ("KEY")
Islands and coral atolls.

**chicle**
A gumlike substance obtained from the latex of certain tropical American trees, such as the sapodilla, used in the making of chewing gum.

**cilantro**
A herb of the parsley family, also called coriander, having strong-scented leaves and used in cooking.

**duendes** ("doo-EN-days")
Mythical dwarves who live in the forests.

**dugu** ("DOO-goo")
A Garifuna ancestral rite, which means Feasting of the Dead. It is held to appease the spirit of a deceased ancestor.

**escabeche** ("ES-kah-BAY-chay")
Also known as ceviche, this dish is prepared by marinating raw seafood in lime or lemon juice.

**gombay** ("gom-BAY")
Drumming and dancing parties held by slaves.

**hickatee** ("hik-ah-TEE")
Central American river turtle.

**jacks**
A type of puff pastry.

**johnnycake**
A flat cake or bread made with cornmeal, usually cooked on a griddle.

**marimba** ("mah-REEM-bah")
A type of xylophone brought to the New World by African slaves, popular among the Maya.

**mauger** ("MAH-ger")
A season of no wind in August.

**milpa** ("MEEL-pah")
A type of farming practiced by the Maya. The jungle is cleared and burned to grow crops for a few years and then left to recover itself.

**Rastafarianism**
A religious sect that regards the late Haile Selassie I of Ethiopia as the Messiah and Africa as the Promised Land.

# BIBLIOGRAPHY

Barry, T. *Inside Belize*. Albuquerque, New Mexico: The Interhemispheric Resource Center, 1995.

Bolland, O. N. *Belize: A New Nation in Central America*. Boulder, Colorado: Westview Press, 1986.

Mahler, R. *Belize: Adventures in Nature*. Santa Fe, New Mexico: John Muir Publications, 1999.

Olson, J. S. *Indians of Central and South America*. Westport, Connecticut: Greenwood Press, 1991.

Sutherland, A. *The Making of Belize: Globalization in the Margins*. Westport, Connecticut: Bergin & Garvey, 1998.

Tenenbaum, B. A., Ed. *Encyclopedia of Latin American History and Culture*. New York: Simon & Schuster Macmillan, 1996.

# INDEX

# INDEX

# INDEX